Renew

PRAISE FOR
Renew

"This devotional book is a fantastic resource for parents seeking to lead their children gently to Jesus. It provides practical application of the timeless gospel principles. You will be blessed."

–Nicole Parker, *mother, author, biblical counselor, speaker*

"Renew brings fresh insights and new perspectives to Bible narratives we know well and have read time and again. The Digging Deeper and Making It Real sections encourage readers to move beyond just passively reading the content to actively applying the insights to their lives."

–Lerone Carson, *mother and children's pastor*

"I appreciate the Renew devotional because it digs deeply into scripture and brings out the applications for me as a parent. It uses a Bible story and goes point by point to capture the application that I need for my day-to-day life. It's definitely a must read!"

–Ruth Yaeger, *mother and writer*

"Renew is relevant. The author draws from a variety of Bible characters and applies their situations to our current world. The author uses fresh examples drawn from recent headlines and our use of social media. Definitely recommend."

–Douglas Pratt, *father, social worker, author*

"The Renew devotions offer a fresh perspective, make me think, and most importantly always point me to Jesus. I love how Merle shares her faith honestly and practically. I look forward to my Renew time with Jesus each week! What a blessing."

–Michelle Coy, *mother and elementary school teacher*

52 WEEKLY DEVOTIONS FOR PARENTS
A Journey through the Bible with a Parenting Perspective

Renew

STAYING WITH JESUS

MERLE POIRIER

My Bible First
HIXSON, TENNESSEE

Copyright © 2022 Merle Poirier. All rights reserved.

Published by My Bible First.

This book or any portion thereof may not be reproduced or used in any manner whatsoever without the express written permission of the publisher except for the use of brief quotations in a book review.

Unless otherwise indicated, all texts are from the New King James Version. Copyright © 1979, 1980, 1982 by Thomas Nelson, Inc. Used by permission. All rights reserved.

Ellen G. White's books and articles referenced in the text may be read at egwwritings.org.

Printed in the United States of America.

Designed by Ellen Musselman
Cover Photo by Lucas Favre on Unsplash
Photography by Unsplash (unsplash.com) and Pexels (pexels.com)

My Bible First
PO Box 536
Hixson, TN 37343
MyBibleFirst.org

startingwithjesus.com/renew

ISBN 9798358838956

Dedication

To my grandsons,
Connor and Justin,
who remind me each day of
the importance of staying with Jesus;

To my husband **Tim**,
who patiently stopped whatever he
was doing to listen to what I had written;

To my daughter **Ellen**,
who not only created the plan,
she helped make it happen;

To my daughter **Lisa**,
whose life experiences
provided so much inspiration; and

Most importantly, to **God**,
who never failed to show up
when I needed Him most.

Table of Contents

Introduction 13

How to Use This Devotional 15

Part One
In the Beginning, God…

Week 1: Our Wonderful God 18

Week 2: Lucifer's Sad Choice 22

Week 3: God's Beautiful Creation 26

Week 4: God's Creation Finished 30

Week 5: God Gives a Very Special Gift 34

Week 6: A Very Sad Day 38

Week 7: Two Brothers Choose 42

Week 8: Noah Builds an Ark 46

Week 9: God's Promise in the Sky 50

Week 10: Foolish Builders 54

Week 11: Selfishness Never Pays 58

Week 12: Angels Rescue Lot 62

Week 13: Abraham and Isaac Trust God 66

Part Two
Learning His Love

Week 14: A Bride for Isaac 72

Week 15: Twins that Weren't Alike 76

Week 16: Jacob's New Name 80

Week 17: Family Problems 84

Week 18: Faithfulness Rewarded 88

Week 19: God Prepares a Deliverer 92

Week 20: God Shows His Power 96

Week 21: Free at Last 100

Week 22: God's Promises at Marah 104

Week 23: Food From Heaven 108

Week 24: Water From a Rock 112

Week 25: God Speaks His Law 116

Week 26: How We Love God 120

Part Three
Following His Plan

Week 27: Remember God's Special Day 126

Week 28: How We Love Others 130

Week 29: Broken Promises 134

Week 30: A Dwelling Place for God 138

Week 31: God's Beautiful Sanctuary 142

Week 32: Nadab and Abihu 146

Week 33: Two Brave Spies 150

Week 34: Rebellion in the Wilderness 154

Week 35: A Sad Mistake 158

Week 36: Balaam, the Greedy Prophet 162

Week 37: The Promised Land at Last 166

Week 38: Blessings and Curses 170

Week 39: The Gibeonites 174

Part Four
Accepting His Call

Week 40: Up and Down Years..180

Week 41: The Call of Gideon 184

Week 42: "Little" Tests 188

Week 43: Samson...192

Week 44: Faithful Ruth..196

Week 45: Hannah's Prayer Answered 200

Week 46: Samuel Hears God's Call 204

Week 47: Angels Guard God's Ark 208

Week 48: Wanting to Be Like Others 212

Week 49: King Saul Becomes Proud 216

Week 50: God Chooses a New King...220

Week 51: David and Goliath 224

Week 52: What Jealousy Does..228

Introduction

Have you ever felt restless? That's where I found myself toward the end of 2020. Always an active volunteer in my church and school, most of those opportunities were no longer available. I felt like I should be doing something with the talents God had given me, but wasn't sure what. One day while talking with my oldest daughter, Ellen, we began to share.

Her burden was the lack of spiritual resources for parents of small children. "You know," she said. "When a parent enters the Beginners' classroom with their first child, they can actually be a member of that class for up to 10 years, depending on how many children they have!" She was speaking of her own experience. While there's nothing wrong with "Jesus loves me" theology, it can lack depth, particularly if you are hungering for more.

As I shared my restlessness, we realized we might be able to help each other. What if we created a devotional for parents that would follow the children's lesson? The parents would already be reading the weekly Bible story with their children. This would simply offer parents a deeper experience. It would be short, accessible, and Ellen added one more thing—"make sure it's a lesson I've never thought of before."

It's a bit of a story to tell, but God closed a series of doors so much so we'd actually given up on the idea. Then about a year later, Ellen had an unexpected conversation

It is my continued prayer that you, the reader, will also find just what you need because God has provided for you.

My Bible First provides resources for children and their parents as a way to encourage families in their walk with Jesus. To see a full list of their products, visit **mybiblefirst.org**.

with a friend from college. This led us to share our idea with the board members of "Starting With Jesus," a ministry focused on helping children to develop a daily relationship with Jesus from a very early age (**startingwithjesus.com**). We received an enthusiastic response. They had been praying for just such a resource! With their help, the devotional project was launched. Each devotional for parents is paired with a children's lesson from the My Bible First curriculum, which follows a three-year overview of the Bible from Genesis to Revelation. This book covers the first year.

Renew first appeared on the Starting With Jesus website in January 2022. I wrote the devotionals. Ellen prepared the graphics and posted them each week. What a pleasure it has been to partner with her. God has used Ellen not only as a cure to my restlessness, but as an advisor, counselor, and gifted designer. She seemed to know just what graphics would make each devotional shine.

It's amazing to have a front row seat to watch God work. I have experienced Him in new ways as I've studied my Bible, wrestling with the high bar Ellen gave me from the beginning—a "new thought" from a familiar story. Yet God has never failed me as He provided something, time and time again. Nor did He fail the readers. One wrote me asking: "Have you been talking to Jesus about my problems? Because every single one of the last few devotionals has been exactly what I needed to hear for the week." I had to smile. I knew God was prompting my thoughts. And I knew He was preparing these devotionals for someone, because I always asked Him to. God knows what others need to hear. It is my continued prayer that you, the reader, will also find just what you need because God has provided for you.

Stay with Jesus and be renewed.

HOW TO USE THIS DEVOTIONAL

Renew was designed to be used with the children's Sabbath School lessons available from My Bible First. Each children's lesson is divided into six parts for parents to study with their child each day of the week. This weekly adult devotional supplements the children's lesson, by offering a deeper study for the parent.

Since Renew began, it has reached beyond young parents finding many others who simply desire a closer walk with Jesus. This book has become something for everyone, and how it is used, is up to you. Since it's a weekly devotional, a lesson can be read in one sitting or you may choose to spread it out through the week.

Each lesson has several parts:
- **Scripture:** The lesson is based off of this portion of scripture. Most lessons, since they are a weekly, have a fairly lengthy Scripture reading.
- **Devotional:** Here is where you will find a thought taken from the Scripture reading to contemplate for the week.
- **Digging Deeper:** Want to go a bit deeper? This section will enhance your understanding of the lesson.
- **Making It Real:** This is for life application. Studying scripture is important, but applying it is vital. Here you will find suggestions on how to bring the lesson into your own life. We might suggest it be read earlier in the week in the event there is a suggestion of things to do during the week.
- **Further Reading:** This is additional reading from *The Bible Story*, a book for children, and the books of Ellen G. White, a Christian author who offers spiritual insight into Bible passages.

Our prayer is that we have offered you a weekly spiritual feast. May you be abundantly blessed as you read through this book this year.

PART ONE

In the Beginning, God...

WEEK ONE

Our Wonderful God

READ **PSALM 139:1-12; PROVERBS 8:22-36**

Psalm 139:1-2 *O Lord, You have searched me and known me. You know my sitting down and my rising up; You understand my thought afar off.*

RENEW YOUR MIND

My husband and I are different when it comes to music. It's not the genre that divides us; it's music versus lyrics. When he hears a song, he hears the music—chords I do not. He can read a book or sleep blissfully with music playing. I cannot. Why? Because all I hear are the lyrics. Yes, I recognize a beautiful tune or memorable melody, but if the lyrics can't be understood or make no sense, I'm done.

Recently I've been reading through the Psalms. Guess what? All lyrics! For whatever reason the Lord saw fit for the music to be forgotten and simply left us the words.

If you haven't read through the Psalms, you should. You will be blessed. These songs will strike a chord in any heart. For me, particularly David's. As I read his psalms, I have learned to recognize his voice.

I am a praying person. I talk with God all the time. We have a relationship, but my conversations with God seem ordinary when reading David's lyrics. His soul is fully present in his laments, as well as his praise. What about me? If I'm honest, I may have a handle on the laments, but my prayers of praise may be lacking.

How is it with you? Do you find your prayers full of asking? Are you one who challenges and reasons in your time with God? Sometimes in the midst of everyday life, our list of what we wish for or want grows. It grabs our attention and our time, while our praise wanes. It's okay. God gets it. You're in good company. David also did his share of complaining. But here's the difference. It's never all that David is. His psalms insert praise either at the beginning, the middle, the end, or all three.

Overwhelmed? Work, kids, or life consuming you? Register your objections with God. He wants you to. But before you start your list, count your blessings first. I know, you've heard it before: *"Count your blessings and suddenly everything will be okay."* No, your problems won't disappear, but your spirit will change. Listing our blessings evokes praise—praise to the One who is there for all our needs. Suddenly your prayers will become psalms, maybe not as poetic as David's, but music to God's ears and yours. And you are renewed.

> **How is it with you? Do you find your prayers full of asking? Are you one who challenges and reasons in your time with God?**

FURTHER READING

Patriarchs and Prophets, pages 33-35

Renew YOUR SPIRIT

make new • restore • replenish • reestablish • revive

DIGGING DEEPER

Of the 150 Psalms, 73 are attributed to David as the author. We know, though, that David actually wrote two more—Psalm 2 and Psalm 95. How do we know? The New Testament speaks of David's authorship and then quotes from these psalms (Acts 4:25 and Heb. 4:7).

> Depending on your circumstances, try reading some of David's words to find sympathy, understanding, and strength as he did in His Creator.

Ellen White, in *Thoughts from the Mount of Blessings*, page 49, credits Psalm 45 to David bringing the total to 76.

The entire book of Psalms has one simple theme: People have problems and God is the solution. While reading all the psalms is something you should plan to do at least once, busy people sometimes need to know where they can find help fast. Depending on your circumstances, try reading some of David's words to find sympathy, understanding, and strength as he did in His Creator.

- Feeling lonely? Read Psalm 25.
- Feeling tired? Read Psalm 6.
- Feeling overwhelmed? Read Psalm 121.
- Lacking confidence? Read Psalm 71.
- Feeling abandon? Read Psalm 22.
- Feeling ignored? Psalm 131.
- Feeling joy? Read Psalm 65.
- Think God no longer hears? Read Psalm 13.
- Want to praise Him? Read Psalm 103.
- Awed by creation? Read Psalm 19.
- Wondering about the future? Read Psalm 27.
- Feeling scared? Read Psalm 23.
- Feeling discouraged? Read Psalm 62.
- Feeling guilty? Read Psalm 130.
- Feeling betrayed? Read Psalm 55.
- Feeling triumphant? Read Psalm 68.

Listing our blessings evokes *praise*.

> **MAKING IT REAL**

1. If you are someone who journals, find time to **make a list of your blessings.** Then use your list to pray a psalm of praise and thanksgiving.

2. Feeling poetic? **Write and sing your own psalm** praising God.

3. Too busy? **While cooking or cleaning, sing a hymn of praise.**

4. **Involve your family at worship time.** Together make a list of your blessings. Then read Psalm 136, inserting your family list in the place of the first line of each verse from 2-25 (if you do the entire psalm, you will need 24 blessings). Read it aloud together.

WEEK TWO

Lucifer's Sad Choice

READ **ISAIAH 14:12-15; EZEKIEL 28:2-19**

Ezekiel 28:17 *"Your heart was lifted up because of your beauty; You corrupted your wisdom for the sake of your splendor."*

RENEW YOUR MIND

At one point in my life, I was fortunate to be a part of a small group of mission-focused people. We worked on projects together and the time shared was friendly and enjoyable. The focus was on the projects, but we enjoyed the typical banter among friends while we worked. Then one day it stopped. I noticed, but assumed people were busy.

Weeks later it came to my attention that someone in our group had suggested ideas about me to the others that were either truth mixed with falsehood or false altogether. The reason for the quiet was not busyness, but purposeful distancing.

The story of Lucifer and his downfall reads similarly. It started simply as expressing his idea of ways to do things better. Gradually it became innuendo, then criticism, then outright falsehood. In the end, all heaven was in an uproar, eventually leading to Lucifer's removal, along with a third of the angels.

To say that my experience was painful is a bit of an understatement. I think what hurt most was that this group who had worked with me for a long time knew what was being said didn't fit what they knew about me but doubted just the same. When it was finally all revealed, one by one the members profusely apologized, saying, "We didn't think it was true, but . . ."

In my situation good, honest people had doubts when someone thought to be trusted whispered what sounded like truth but was, in actuality, far from it. What is harder to believe, is that this same thing happened in heaven, but about God. That heaven could be torn apart by accusation and lies seems impossible, and yet it was.

Focusing on Satan and his schemes will never bring encouragement. He only peddles despair, disruption, and discouragement. But if we lift our sights in this

from Lucifer to God, we recognize what we will always find—love. How long the conflict lasted, we do not know. We know it moved from heaven to earth. What did not change from then to now is the supreme love God has for His creation, whether angels or people. Love, so strong that to save us, He sent His Son to die so we can experience eternity with Him. And when this is our focus, we are renewed.

FURTHER READING

Patriarchs and Prophets, pages 35-43

The Story of Redemption, pages 13-19

Renew YOUR SPIRIT

make new • restore • replenish • reestablish • revive

DIGGING DEEPER

When we think of heaven, we think happy thoughts. We like the idea of visiting other worlds, riding giraffes, wearing crowns, and on it goes. But further study reveals there may be another dimension we need to consider.

> [Angels] know the complete and overwhelming sadness that comes when someone you know and love, suddenly and unexpectedly turns against all they've ever believed.

"Good angels weep to hear the words of Satan, and to see how he despises to follow the direction of Christ, their exalted and loving commander" (*Spiritual Gifts*, vol. 3, p. 37). Weep? Weeping suggests overwhelming sadness, an element that doesn't match our idea of heaven, does it?

It is said that angels cannot identify with the human experience because they have not known sin or the salvation we count so precious. Certainly, the full expression of this is true. But angels do understand betrayal. They know hurt. They know the complete and overwhelming sadness that comes when someone you know and love, suddenly and unexpectedly turns against all they've ever believed. Loss. Disappointment. Unfaithfulness. Not quite the angel experience we might imagine.

Heaven *is* a happy place. It can't be anything less, because the presence of God is there along with Jesus, our Redeemer, Creator, and Friend. But this happiness doesn't mean there will never be sadness or weeping because of sin—sin that started in heaven and extended to this world. Weeping isn't just an earthly experience, it's a heavenly one, too. But in the midst of sadness, no matter the cause, we can still do what the angels did. Go to Jesus. Bask in the presence of your heavenly Father. Sing a song of praise. Then one day, our tears like theirs, will be dried by the hand of God Himself as we look forward to an eternity of happiness in heaven.

God's love will never change.

MAKING IT REAL

1. **Have you ever had someone betray you? Disappoint you?** Cause you hurt? How did you handle it? How does having a loving Savior to turn to make a difference?

2. **Is there a hurt you need to turn over to Jesus?** Take a step in that direction today.

WEEK THREE

God's Beautiful Creation

READ **GENESIS 1:1-23; PSALM 33:6-9; JOHN 1:1-3**

Genesis 1:2 *The earth was without form, and void; and darkness was on the face of the deep. And the Spirit of God was hovering over the face of the waters.*

RENEW YOUR MIND

One doesn't start building a house with the roof. One doesn't start a story with the ending. We start at the beginning.

This, too, is how Genesis begins. "In the beginning God created the heavens and the earth." Linger here a moment as we imagine Creation.

Form pictures in your mind as we watch the beginning unfold. There is no form, only darkness. Light begins to pierce through the blackness. A horizon appears separating the sky from the water. The waters gather together, and dry land appears. "And God saw that it was good."

Good? This is not unlike Michelangelo looking at a block of marble, Handel contemplating his harpsichord, or DaVinci staring at a blank canvas. At this point there is only time, weather, and foundation. No splash of color. No interesting details. Yet God pronounces it good. Why? Because God sees what will be.

"Nowhere was there even a blade of grass or clinging lichen. Yet it seemed good to its Maker, who could see it in relation to the uses for which He had made it, and as a fit preparatory step to the new wonders He was going to introduce" (*Seventh-day Adventist Bible Commentary*, vol. 1, p. 212).

The newborn who won't sleep, the toddler who resists toilet training, the awkward middle schooler, the challenging teenager, the young adult who cannot find their path, the mature adult whose path is less than they imagined, the senior whose life, health, and future are uncertain—all are in progress. God sees lives as Michelangelo saw David in a block of marble, Handel heard a symphony, and DaVinci saw a Mona Lisa. God sees you, His creation, in preparation for His purpose for your life.

Are you discouraged? Disheartened? Having difficulty seeing your next step? Wondering how you will survive this moment you are in? Do not despair. Your sight is limited. It's what sin brings to our world. What God sees, though, is an opening to the wonder He will introduce. You are His creation. You have a purpose. Trust in Him. You may see only a blank canvas or a wobbly foundation. The color is lacking. The details unclear. But God sees you, and what He sees, is good.

> Do not despair. Your sight is limited. It's what sin brings to our world. What God sees, though, is an opening to the wonder He will introduce.

FURTHER READING

Patriarchs and Prophets, page 44

The Story of Redemption, page 20

The Bible Story, vol. 1, pages 13-34

Renew YOUR SPIRIT

make new • restore • replenish • reestablish • revive

DIGGING DEEPER

Genesis 1:1 tell us how the earth began and reminds us of the importance of beginnings. While we as humans are finite, with both a beginning and an end, God is without beginning and end. Remind yourself of our infinite and eternal God by reading these scriptures.*

1. **Hebrews 1:10-12; Psalm 90: 2, 10.** While we as humans, have a beginning and an end, our Creator is infinite.
2. **Colossians 1:18; John 1:1-3.** God is the beginning.
3. **Psalm 111:10; James 1: 17.** All things have their beginning with Him.
4. **Genesis 1:26, 27; John 3:5; 1 John 3:1-3.** Our lives must find a new beginning in Him.
5. **Philippians 1:6.** We find assurance in this promise: ". . . that He who has begun a good work in you will complete it until the day of Jesus Christ . . ."
6. **Hebrews 12:2.** Our God will see us through. He is "the author and finisher of our faith."

> While we as humans are finite, with both a beginning and an end, God is without beginning and end.

*Seventh-day Adventist Bible Commentary, vol. 1, p. 207.

"Christ can look upon the misery of the world without a shade of sorrow for having created man. In the human heart He sees more than sin, more than misery. In His infinite wisdom and love He sees man's possibilities, the height to which he may attain. He knows that, even though human beings have abused their mercies and destroyed their God-given dignity, yet the Creator is to be glorified in their redemption" (*Thoughts from the Mount of Blessings*, pp. vii, viii).

You are His creation.
You have a purpose.
Trust in Him.

MAKING IT REAL

The best way to revel in God's creative power is to be out in nature. Granted, you may be reading this during the cold months of winter, but there is still much to be seen and felt by spending time outdoors.

1. **Take a walk** even if it means bundling up. As you walk, what can you discover that demonstrates God's goodness? His power? His strength?
2. How can learning about creation **help you trust God more?**
3. Unable to get outside? **Look out your window.** What can you see? How does it make you think of God?
4. **Watch a nature video.** As you do let the Holy Spirit fill your soul with affirmation: God sees the potential of your life, and "it is good."

WEEK FOUR

God's Creation Finished

> **READ** **GENESIS 1:24-2:1; GENESIS 2:7; PSALM 8:4,5**

Genesis 1:27 *So God created man in His own image; in the image of God He created him; male and female He created them.*

> **RENEW YOUR MIND**

My daughter recently gave birth to our second grandson. I spent time with him just this evening before sitting down to write. He's three days old and completely perfect. Smooth baby skin, chubby cheeks, silky blonde hair, and tiny feet with toes that curl around your finger.

Just as my grandson becomes more like his father because of the time he spends with him, may we too spend so much time with Jesus that people can't help but see the resemblance.

As I stared into his sleepy face, those little eyes squinting now and again at the bright lights around him, I wondered who he looks like. He's quite different looking than his older brother. When he was born, it was as if I gazed into the face of his mother years earlier. But this little guy isn't one that stirs my memory, but maybe his other grandmother will see what I do not—the sleepy face she rocked 30-plus years ago.

Genesis 1:26 says, "Then God said, "Let Us make man in Our image, according to Our likeness . . ." Adam and Eve were made in the image of God. Not only to look like their Creator, but to share His attributes as well.

My older grandson is a wonderful mix of both his father and his mother. While he may look like his mother, he has the interests and passions of his father. His joy in finding a worm or toad, his interest in all things nature, comes from spending time with his dad. Because of the time spent with his father, he has become like his father.

We are also made in the image of God. While sin may obscure what Adam and Eve initially experienced, through Christ's light and glory we may reflect our Creator. I remember listening to an Amy Grant song called "My Father's Eyes," expressing hope that when people saw her, they'd see she looked like her Father, her heavenly Father.

Just as my grandson becomes more like his father because of the time he spends with him, may we too spend so much time with Jesus that people can't help but see the resemblance. And when we reflect and share the love of Jesus, others are renewed.

FURTHER READING

Patriarchs and Prophets, pages 44-51

The Story of Redemption, pages 20-23

The Bible Story, vol. 1, pages 35-56

Renew YOUR SPIRIT

make new • restore • replenish • reestablish • revive

DIGGING DEEPER

Genesis 1:26 describes the creation of man in plural terms. "Then God said, "Let *Us* make man in *Our* image, according to *Our* likeness . . ." The word "us" indicates the presence of at least one other entity in the creation process. This strong evidence of the Godhead is found immediately, in the very first chapter of the Bible.

> God the Father, God the Son, and the Holy Spirit, all three, fully present and deeply involved in the creation of this world, and most specifically in the making of man, their crowning achievement.

Verse 2 of the same chapter reveals that the Spirit of God hovered over the waters. Later we find the presence of Christ clearly identified in the New Testament (John 1:1-3, 14) as a participant in the making of man. God the Father, God the Son, and the Holy Spirit, all three, fully present and deeply involved in the creation of this world, and most specifically in the making of man, their crowning achievement.

While we do not know exactly what being made in the image of God means, we do know that Adam resembled God in his character (*Patriarchs and Prophets*, p. 45). Six thousand years have passed since that day, but we, too, can still reflect the image of God like Adam, perhaps not physically, but in our lives and service to Him, who as Paul said, "for in Him we live and move and have our being" (Acts 17:28).

MAKING IT REAL

Make a list of the **character attributes of Jesus.**
How can you be more like Jesus?

May we spend so much time with Jesus that people can't help but see *the resemblance.*

WEEK FIVE

God Gives a Very Special Gift

> **READ** GENESIS 2:1-3; EXODUS 20:8-11; ISAIAH 58:13, 14; 66:22, 23

Genesis 2:3 Then God blessed the seventh day and sanctified it, because in it He rested from all His work which God had created and made.

> **RENEW YOUR MIND**

I sometimes think about what it would be like if I were not a Sabbath-keeper. I shudder at the thought. My days are full morning to night. Having an "off switch," is a necessity. When Sabbath comes around especially if it has been a stressful week, the laundry can mock, the clutter can taunt, but I am not guilted into action for I have an excuse: I am resting. Is that what Sabbath is? Perhaps.

I once had the opportunity to visit Michelangelo's statue of "David" in Florence, Italy. I lingered by the sculpture for some time simply savoring its magnificence. Is that what God did on that first Sabbath of Creation? Is it what He expects me to do? Perhaps.

Adam and Eve labored in Eden tending the garden. Work for them, though, is a relative term since sin had yet to enter their world. Imagine tending a garden in a perfect climate with no bugs, sweat, thorns, or rocks to impede your toil. Why would the first humans need rest?

Ellen White writes, "God saw that a Sabbath was essential for man, even in Paradise. He needed to lay aside his own interests and pursuits for one day of the seven, that he might more fully contemplate the works of God and meditate upon His power and goodness. He needed a Sabbath to remind him more vividly of God and to awaken gratitude because all that he enjoyed and possessed came from the beneficent hand of the Creator" (*Patriarchs and Prophets*, p. 48).

Ah, now we understand. While Sabbath may be a time to stop our work, a time to discover the joys of nature, God's real intention, even in Eden, was about contemplating God, and more specifically "to awaken gratitude."

If honest, we will reluctantly admit that the busyness of life is completely absorbing and totally distracting. We can have days when we hit the ground running from our beds and run nonstop until we crawl back into it at the end of the day. When that happens, it isn't that we are ungrateful, but we are just too busy to stop long enough to linger, to pause, to do what I did in Florence by the sculpture. We need to stop long enough to be grateful for what God has done for us.

This Sabbath, make time to remember. Make time to ponder. Make time to think vividly of God. And as you awaken gratitude toward Him, you will be renewed.

Make time to think vividly of God.

FURTHER READING

Patriarchs and Prophets, pages 47-48, 111-116

The Bible Story, vol. 1, pages 57-60

Renew YOUR SPIRIT

make new • restore • replenish • reestablish • revive

DIGGING DEEPER

We automatically think of rest associated with Sabbath as the absence of labor. We find things to do together on the Sabbath, because work and school no longer divide us. But one important element is sometimes overlooked—worship. Consider this interesting meaning of Sabbath shared to me by a pastor friend:

> Sabbath is a day when man and woman dwell together in the house of the Father.

Shabbath = man and woman
Shabbath = *Shebet*, which means dwell together
Shabbath = *Beth*, which means house
Shabbath = *Abba*, which means Father

Put it all together: Sabbath is a day when man and woman dwell together in the house of the Father.

MAKING IT REAL

In the past four lessons, we have learned about praise, love, power, and gratitude. Find ways to incorporate these into your Sabbath:

Praise: Sing hymns for family worship that particularly bring smiles to the faces of your family.

Love: On your own or with your family, write a love note to God. Then create a special card with a message of love, and mail it this week to someone.

Power: It's time to find God in nature. If you can go outside for a walk in the woods or by the ocean, do so. If not, find a video of waterfalls or the Grand Canyon or something really amazing and powerful in nature.

Gratitude: Attend a worship service today. If you can, meet with like-minded believers in person. As you sing, pray, and listen to the Word, do so with a grateful heart.

We need to *stop long enough* to be grateful for what God has done for us.

WEEK SIX

A Very Sad Day

READ **GENESIS 2:8-17; 3**

Genesis 3:10 *"I heard Your voice in the garden, and I was afraid because I was naked; and I hid myself."*

RENEW YOUR MIND

I don't know about you, but when I read the story of Adam and Eve, I cannot help but feel anger, sadness, and frustration. If only they had listened to the warnings given by God, the world wouldn't be as it is. Why couldn't they simply obey?

And then, obviously, I realize that the same question can be repeated today. What happened then, happens now. Sin is always at the door, knocking for entrance in enticing ways. Studying their story, helps our story.

Ellen White reveals something interesting: "Eve had been perfectly happy by her husband's side in her Eden home; but, like restless modern Eves, she was flattered with the hope of entering a higher sphere than that which God had assigned her. In attempting to rise above her original position, she fell far below it. A similar result will be reached by all who are unwilling to take up cheerfully their life duties in accordance with God's plan. In their efforts to reach positions for which He has not fitted them, many are leaving vacant the place where they might be a blessing. In their desire for a higher sphere, many have sacrificed true womanly dignity and nobility of character, and have left undone the very work that Heaven appointed them" (*Patriarchs and Prophets,* p. 59).

These are strong words and may touch close to home. I doubt anyone reading this has not felt restlessness; the desire for something (or someone) better. Satan lured Eve with flattery, and then followed quickly with a suggestion of dissatisfaction. Once convinced that her situation could be better, it was an easy step to accept forbidden fruit.

We aren't that far away from what happened in Eden, are we? How easy are we complimented? How quickly do we compare? How much time does it take to become dissatisfied with our home, our job, our life, our situation? Each of these takes us away from what God has planned for us. Only He knows what will truly make us happy. Only in His guidance will we attain true worth and satisfaction. Only in God is there a cure for our restlessness. Seek Him. Find Him. And when you do, you will be renewed.

In their efforts to reach positions for which He has not fitted them, many are leaving vacant the place where they might be a blessing.

FURTHER READING

Patriarchs and Prophets, pages 52-62

The Story of Redemption, pages 24-41

The Bible Story, vol. 1, pages 61-72

Renew YOUR SPIRIT

make new • restore • replenish • reestablish • revive

DIGGING DEEPER

The counterbalance to the frustration we might feel about Adam and Eve's serious error in judgment, is the amazing plan of salvation that God and His Son, Jesus, created for them and us. This is encapsulated best in John 3:16. One commentator summed it up this way:*

> God and His Son, Jesus, created an amazing plan of salvation for Adam and Eve, and us.

God	The Almighty Authority
So loved the world	The Mightiest Motive
That He gave His only begotten Son	The Greatest Gift
That whosoever	The Widest Welcome
Believes in Him	The Easiest Escape
Should not perish	The Divine Deliverance
But have everlasting life	The Priceless Possession

*David Guzik, enduringword.com

MAKING IT REAL

Mrs. White draws back the curtain allowing us to "see" what transpired in heaven as a response to sin (*The Story of Redemption*, p. 42). Jesus approached His Father three times before He emerged with the plan of salvation. This was no easy decision on the part of God the Father. To save us, He must sacrifice His only Son. When you realize that God gave Him for that purpose, how does that help you understand God's love for man? In what way does that help you understand God's love for you individually?

Only in God
is there a cure for
our restlessness.

WEEK SEVEN

Two Brothers Choose

READ **GENESIS 4:1-16**

Genesis 4:4, 5 *And the Lord respected Abel and his offering, but He did not respect Cain and his offering.*

RENEW YOUR MIND

The story of Cain and Abel is one we know well. But it's entirely possible that our familiarity with the story causes us to miss a greater point. While we easily identify disobedience followed by murder in this story, there is perhaps a more subtle message within the text.

The Hebrew word used here for offering is *minchah*, which covers any type of gift an individual could bring to God. This word extends to animal sacrifices or first fruits—usually grain, but could extend to garden produce. If both types of offerings are acceptable, what was the problem with Cain's offering? It was twofold.

First, it appears that the offering brought by Abel and Cain was for atonement, a time of confession of sin as well as honoring God as the only One who can forgive sins. Scripture doesn't reveal the purpose, but Abel's offering implies the offering required the shedding of blood. Only the shedding of blood can atone for sins (Lev. 17:11).

Now look at verse 4. "The Lord respected Abel . . . ." Abel is listed first, then his offering. What this suggests is that while offerings are important, the motivation of the giver is even more valued by heaven. Maybe you remember the story of Saul and Samuel: "Behold, to obey is better than sacrifice, and to heed than the fat of rams" (1 Samuel 15:22).

Abel's offering was brought in faith and obedience. His desire was to worship as God required, recognizing his need of forgiveness because he was a sinner. Cain, on the other hand, did what was asked, but only halfway. He determined in his heart to take God's plan and modify it. In so doing he formed his own salvation plan. He brought an offering of his own works, one that did not show recognition of himself as a sinner in need of God.

Sacrificing lambs versus the gift of produce feels a bit removed from us today. We don't have to make such decisions or do we? Cain's religion was an empty one. He was simply going through the motions. But before we become too judgmental of Cain, we should recognize that we can also be half-hearted Christians. *Go to church.* Check. *Read my Bible.* Check. *Pray before meals.* Check. It all feels good and right. But if Jesus is not at the center of why we do what we do, our religion may be empty as well. It's not about our sacrifice, but about our heart. Let us plan each day to come to Jesus whole-heartedly giving completely of ourselves in worship and recognition of our deep need of a Savior. It is only in this way we are renewed.

> He determined in his heart to take God's plan and modify it.

FURTHER READING

Patriarchs and Prophets, pages 63-79

The Story of Redemption, pages 42-56

The Bible Story, vol. 1, pages 73-90

Renew YOUR SPIRIT

make new • restore • replenish • reestablish • revive

DIGGING DEEPER

Some interesting discoveries are found in the story of Cain and Abel.

- When Eve held her first newborn son in her arms, Eve named him "Qayin" (Cain). The full meaning of his name is "I have gotten a man, the Lord." Eve saw the Messiah in her arms. Her hope of reversing the curse given in Genesis 3:15 had materialized or so she thought.

> Abel lives up to his name for he sees in himself nothing worthy without his Savior. One might wonder if Cain's attitude may have come from having to live up to expectations that were unfairly imposed upon him.

- Interestingly, when the second son arrives, he is given the name, Abel, which means "vanity" or "nothingness." Let the full meaning of that sink in. In a sense Abel lives up to his name for he sees in himself nothing worthy without his Savior. One might wonder if Cain's attitude may have come from having to live up to expectations that were unfairly imposed upon him.

- Note that when Cain complains to God after Abel is killed, his complaint is about his punishment, not of his sin, giving a clearer insight into his attitude toward spiritual things.

- Cain's punishment was a further expansion of Adam's. When Adam and Eve sinned, they were sent out of the Garden of Eden. Cain is sent even farther away from where the descendants of Eden lived. Adam had to till the soil and it was challenging. The land, the thing Cain loved most, was resistant to anything he could try to produce.

It's not about *your sacrifice,* but about your heart.

MAKING IT REAL

When Abel brought his lamb, it was one lamb for one man. Later, at the Passover, it was one lamb for a family. At the tabernacle on the Day of Atonement, it was one lamb for the nation. With Jesus, it is one Lamb who takes away the sin of the entire world (John 1:29)*.

Fortunately, we don't have to make animal sacrifices today. Jesus took our sins once and for all, making a way for our salvation. This amazing gift of love is one we should embrace every day. Sacrifices, though, are part of the Christian walk. What sacrifices do you make in order to be a Christian? Do you find these difficult? If so, what are ways to make the Christian life easier for yourself and for others?

*Adapted from David Guzik, enduringword.com

WEEK EIGHT

Noah Builds an Ark

READ **GENESIS 5-7**

Genesis 6:2 *The sons of God saw the daughters of men, that they were beautiful; and they took wives for themselves of all whom they chose.*

RENEW YOUR MIND

Have you ever sat in an inner tube and floated on the water? You lay on your back, staring at the blue sky, the clouds are puffy and white, and the water gently rocks you back and forth. It's relaxing, enjoyable, and seemingly harmless.

> **Eventually they spent more time in the valley than on the mountaintop. They lost their sensitivity to sin. They had drifted slowly and steadily away from God.**

Imagine, though, if the water you're floating on has a steep waterfall ahead. You're aware of it. You've heard about it, but it's far away, and nothing to worry about. So, you dangle your feet in the water, drag your fingers along the surface watching the clouds go by, never realizing that it's not just the clouds that are drifting, it's you.

The descendants of Seth didn't plan to leave God. They lived on the mountain away from the Cainites in the valley. They loved righteousness more than pleasure. They worshiped God. They were sure in their choices. At first, they only visited the valley. When they did, it was enjoyable, and the company was pleasant. Eventually they spent more time in the valley than on the mountaintop. They lost their sensitivity to sin. They had drifted slowly and steadily away from God.

The valley can do that to us. We get busy, bored, restless, or relaxed, and we drift away in small and subtle ways. Our morning devotionals are interrupted until they aren't happening. Our evening prayers get cut short because we're so tired, we fall asleep while praying. The sermon is heard, but we have no idea what was said because our minds wandered, or our eyes were distracted. These are all small things that happen to everyone, but added together they inch us away from God, not toward.

Being an active and engaged Christian is not easy. It involves intentionality. It involves commitment. It involves assessment. Sin drift happens to the best of us. Take a moment and ask yourself: Where am I? On the mountaintop? Or drifting toward the valley? Remember, it is on the mountaintop where you find God and are renewed.

FURTHER READING

Patriarchs and Prophets, pages 80-104

The Story of Redemption, pages 57-69

The Bible Story, vol. 1, pages 91-115

Renew YOUR SPIRIT

make new • restore • replenish • reestablish • revive

DIGGING DEEPER

Sin reached a point where God determined to start again. Noah was commissioned to build an ark to the specifications that God gave him.

The ark took 120 years to build. During that time, Noah not only directed the building, but he also preached. God had told him what He had planned to do, and Noah urgently and persistently preached this to the people.

> The ark took 120 years to build. During that time, Noah not only directed the building, but he also preached. God had told him what He had planned to do, and Noah urgently and persistently preached this to the people.

Ellen White reveals that he actually did make an impression. "A multitude at first apparently received the warning of Noah, yet did not fully turn to God with true repentance. There was some time given them before the Flood was to come, in which they were to be placed upon probation—to be proved and tried. They failed to endure the trial. The prevailing degeneracy overcame them, and they finally joined others who were corrupt in deriding and scoffing at faithful Noah" (*The Story of Redemption*, p. 64).

When the flood did come, man and beast alike were frantic. Complete chaos reigned as thunderclouds gathered, lightening bolts hurled toward the earth targeted homes, gardens, idols. As the water climbed higher and higher, Mrs. White records a sad commentary: "They called upon Him earnestly, but His ear was not open to their cry" (*The Story of Redemption*, p. 67). How heartbreaking! How difficult it is to imagine a time and place where God is no longer inclined to hear the cries of people.

Jesus tells us, "As it was in the days of Noah, so it will be also in the days of the Son of Man. . . . Even so will it be in the day when the Son of Man is revealed." (Luke 17:26, 30). So similar days are coming. May we fully be ready when Jesus comes again.

Faith is *waiting for rain* when there are no clouds.

MAKING IT REAL

The people in the days of Noah were completely convinced by what they could see. The sun was shining; there was no threat of water coming from the sky, a completely unheard of experience. The earth, then, still retained much of its Eden-like appearance. And yet what they failed to recognize was the invisible—the God they had rejected or even Satan who did all in his power to help them continue in their wretchedness.

Think about this great controversy between good and evil that is still ongoing today. In what ways can you see the invisible force of good in your life? How is God impacting you? Make a list and fasten it on your bathroom mirror for one week. Each morning read it to remind you of the goodness we sometimes fail to recognize in a world that continues to bombard our senses.

WEEK NINE

God's Promise in the Sky

> **READ** **GENESIS 8; 9:1-17**

Genesis 9:13 *"I set My rainbow in the cloud, and it shall be for the sign of the covenant between Me and the earth."*

> **RENEW YOUR MIND**

My husband and I met through enterprising church friends who thought we'd make a good match. Subsequently we would find ourselves at the same house for Sabbath dinner or squeezed next to each other in the same pew. We had caught on to them, but not yet to each other, when it was decided (also by them) that he should follow me as we drove to a church campout.

That ride was one of the most memorable we've ever taken as we found ourselves literally driving directly into the end of a rainbow. This was before the age of cellphones, so we experienced it together but separately, unable to express the awe of color shining in front and around us.

Needless to say, when we planned our wedding we made the theme about the rainbow. The colors we chose (pastel, not primary), and our custom-made invitation invited our friends and family to watch us covenant our love as God had covenanted His. One of my daughters while looking at the pictures from that day said, "You couldn't do that today."

Unfortunately, she's right. The rainbow today is less about God's love, and more about symbolizing sexual preference, the loss of beloved pets, the birth of a child after a miscarriage, or healthcare workers in a crisis. The human race has managed to take one of God's most beautiful signs and make it about us.

Ellen White had a similar experience viewing a rainbow as my husband and I. Afterwards she wrote: "As we look upon this bow, the seal and sign of God's promise to man, that the tempest of His wrath should no more desolate our world by the waters of a flood, we contemplate that other than finite eyes are looking upon this glorious sight. Angels rejoice as they gaze upon this precious token of God's love to man. The world's Redeemer looks upon it; for it was through His instrumentality that this bow was made to appear in the heavens, as a token or covenant of promise to man. God Himself looks upon the bow in the clouds and remembers His everlasting covenant between Himself and man" (*Our High Calling*, p. 314).

The first time I read that I was amazed. I thought rainbows were for me—a comforting reminder that rain will end with no cataclysmic circumstances. But the rainbow is so much more—it is a tie that binds heaven and earth together. We remember. All heaven remembers. And together we are renewed.

Angels rejoice as they gaze upon this precious token of God's love to man.

FURTHER READING

Patriarchs and Prophets, pages 105-110

The Story of Redemption, pages 69-71

The Bible Story, vol. 1, pages 116-123

Renew YOUR SPIRIT

make new • restore • replenish • reestablish • revive

DIGGING DEEPER

Two interesting points can be understood from the flood story.

1. Embedded in the flood story is the understanding of waiting on God. Review the timings in the Bible text of the flood story. Noah removes the covering of the ark and sees that the ground is dry (Gen. 8:13). The next step after that is leaving the ark itself (verses 14-16). Note that the time elapsed between those verses is almost two months! This is a strong illustration of faith, patience, and obedience. From all Noah could see there was no reason not to leave the ark, yet God does not open the door. Instead of complaining, imagining work-arounds, or somehow crawling out the top, they wait for God's timing even when it might appear that God had simply forgotten them. Something to remember next time you are waiting.

2. There is a strong parallel between the opening chapters of Genesis (1-3) and the flood story (6-9). The flood creates a watery chaos, just as in Genesis 1 where we find the earth covered in water. The flood water is blown by wind (8:1), just as the water on the surface of the deep in creation is acted upon by the Spirit of God. After the waters receded from the flood, dry land appears, and God brings forth Noah, his family, and the animals. In the Creation story God brings forth the animals by their families as well as man. The flood essentially is a re-creation story. God beginning again. Out of the chaos comes God's plan.

> From all Noah could see there was no reason not to leave the ark, yet God does not open the door. Instead of complaining, imagining work-arounds, or somehow crawling out the top, they wait for God's timing even when it might appear that God had simply forgotten them.

Out of the chaos comes *God's plan.*

MAKING IT REAL

We are promised that God will never destroy the world again by flood. Jesus, however, compares the last days to be like Noah (Matt. 24:37). So, we know this life will end when Jesus comes. A devastation is coming. Not another flood, but the ending of sin.

Those who lived prior to the flood were unconvinced by Noah's preaching. Some believed for a while, but eventually followed the crowd. We must begin now to shore ourselves up with truth. We must study our Bibles diligently, seek a life of prayer, and ask for discernment and strength as this world grows steadily more wicked.

Jesus *is* coming again. Do not study the story of Noah and the flood with your children or casually read through Genesis without heeding the warnings. Those given then are the same now. Be ready. Be ready. Be ready. He's coming soon.

WEEK TEN

Foolish Builders

READ **GENESIS 11:1-9**

Genesis 11:4 *And they said, "Come, let us build ourselves a city, and a tower whose top is in the heavens."*

RENEW YOUR MIND

If you were to visit an ancient walled city, there is a good chance you might see a strong tower rising from the wall. It served as a watchtower for approaching enemies or as a place of refuge. Major cities of the world boast towers—skyscrapers of amazing architectural genius and beauty. On the coast or on the dusty plains there may be a weather tower looming into the sky to watch and study approaching storms.

Watch. Protect. Attract. Study. All these were reasons to build the Tower of Babel. "Come, let us build ourselves a city, and a tower . . . " (Gen. 11:4). Seems fairly harmless, until you understand the motive. Let's finish the verse: " . . . whose top is in the heavens; let us make a name for ourselves, lest we be scattered abroad over the face of the whole earth."

The ark story finishes in chapter 9 with God giving a directive and a promise. The promise we seem to remember easily—the rainbow that signifies that God will never destroy the world again with a flood. The directive, we sometimes miss: "Be fruitful and multiply, and fill the earth" (Gen. 9:1). It would appear that those living then, also forgot. Instead of scattering over the earth, they did the opposite—built a magnificent tower that would become a wonder of the world, concentrating everyone in one place. In addition, if built high enough, it would save them from another worldwide flood. For both these reasons and more, this tower was in opposition to God.

Building the tower wasn't the problem. It was what it represented. We, too, can make similar decisions. No, we aren't building physical towers, but we do sometimes attempt to provide for our own safety, to imagine our own importance, to become so independent we have no need of anyone, especially God. We don't do it intentionally as perhaps they did, but if honest, we know that we may have comparable tendencies.

The only tower in our lives is found in Psalm 61:3: "For you [God] have been a shelter for me, a strong tower from the enemy." There is no need to build. No need to boast. Only to shelter in the shadow of the fortress we know as Jesus. In that place, we are renewed.

> We aren't building physical towers, but we do sometimes attempt to provide for our own safety, to imagine our own importance, to become so independent we have no need of anyone, especially God.

FURTHER READING

Patriarchs and Prophets, pages 117-124

The Story of Redemption, pages 72-74

The Bible Story, vol. 1, pages 124-130

Renew YOUR SPIRIT

make new • restore • replenish • reestablish • revive

DIGGING DEEPER

Let's compare and contrast the Creation story followed by the rebellion of Cain, with the flood story followed by the Tower of Babel.

Last week we saw the parallel of God creating the world to the flood story where the world is "re-created."

> Where wickedness was allowed to grow in generations before the flood, God now steps in and scatters the people.

After the flood, there is a separation of the descendants of Noah. Ellen White reveals three distinct groups (*The Story of Redemption*, p. 72). The first group obeyed God. The second group chose not to believe in God at all, devising an explanation for how and why the flood happened. The last group believed in God and the account of the flood, but they were angry at God. Just as Cain's descendants drifted away from the Sethites, there is a separation of those in rebellion against God and those who feared Him.

They moved to the plain, just as the Cainites moved to the valley. The idea to build the tower was born out of full rebellion against God. They built beautiful homes within its walls, lived in excess and abandon, exalting themselves higher and higher both literally and figuratively. Where wickedness was allowed to grow in generations before the flood, God now steps in and scatters the people.

Multiplying languages has long-lasting reverberations even down to our day. God's directive to fill the earth was fulfilled, but at a high cost. The original plan was that God's truth, and His story would be shared around the earth. But because of the people's rebellion, this became difficult as languages and dialects multiplied.

Spreading the gospel around the world is challenging in many respects, but one major cause is the variety of languages. Did you know that India alone has more than 19,500 languages and dialects? Amazing. So, you can see there is a need for translators, missionaries, and financial means to share God's love to everyone. While God's solution caused evil to be spread more slowly, it came at a price.

Shelter in the shadow of the fortress we know as *Jesus*.

MAKING IT REAL

Towers are not all bad. It's at the top of a tower that we can often see more clearly where we are. The same can be true of a mountain. Spend time in your worship, thinking about mountains. Here's a couple ideas:

1. **How many Bible stories can you relate** that have to do with a mountain?
2. If you're able, **memorize Psalm 121:1-8.** If that seems a bit overwhelming, memorize just verses 1 and 2.
3. **Sing "Higher Ground"** (#625, *Seventh-day Adventist Hymnal*) for worship. If you do not have a hymnal, visit **sdahymnal.org**.

WEEK ELEVEN

Selfishness Never Pays

> **READ** **GENESIS 11:27-32; 12-14**

Genesis 13:11 Then Lot chose for himself all the plain of Jordan, and Lot journeyed east.

> **RENEW YOUR MIND**

Genesis 11 through 14 is jam-packed with Bible truth. These chapters include lessons about stepping out in faith, honoring aging parents, witnessing, the adverse effects of lying, the consequences of selfish choices, and tithing. Wow! So, which morsel do we choose as the one take-away when the entire banquet is so inviting?

It would seem the best place to settle is with Lot. Or is it? He wasn't a bad person, but Lot's long range vision wasn't what it could be. In that, many of us may be like him. We make life choices without considering the long view. When we drive, we don't look at the front of the car, we look far ahead. Why? Because if we drove the car simply looking at the front of the car, we'd end up in a ditch or someone else's backseat. Life is also like that, or it should be. Lot chose what he could see directly in front of him—the more favorable land. It looked better; the grass was greener; life was easier.

Notice that in the space of a few chapters, Lot moves toward Sodom, then he's near Sodom, then he's in Sodom, and finally, we find him sitting at the gate with the leaders. One seemingly innocent choice ended Lot in a place where he was not only surrounded by wickedness, but he learned to be comfortable with "Sodom" thinking. How do we know? Because when confronted by a wicked mob demanding evil things, Lot's compromise was to give them his daughters instead! Later, his daughters thought of an even worse example of "Sodom thinking."

Are we, like Lot, content with "Sodom" thinking? Satan is cunning. He knows that if he puts evil right in front of us, we'd reject it immediately.

However, if allowed to be exposed gradually in what we wear, eat, entertainment, friends, and more, is it possible to slowly drift toward "Sodom" not recognizing that we've actually moved? Is it also possible that while we might recognize the shift, we've become so comfortable that we don't see as we once did, but with new lenses?

Where we place our tent, where we choose to settle, completely dictates our decisions. Choose to camp with God, even if it isn't in the best territory with the best view. Let us pitch our tents, tie down our stakes, and brace ourselves against all that might blow against us. We are not alone, but with God. Remember to look heavenward, count the stars, and be renewed. Ⓡ

> Where we place our tent, where we choose to settle, completely dictates our decisions.

FURTHER READING

Patriarchs and Prophets, pages 125-136

The Bible Story, vol. 1, pages 133-155

Renew YOUR SPIRIT

make new • restore • replenish • reestablish • revive

DIGGING DEEPER

When Lot chose to move toward Sodom, he moved towards the east. This is the fourth time moving toward the east is characterized as moving away from God (Genesis 3:24, 4:16, 11:2). Adam and Eve move east of the garden, Cain moves east to the valley, descendants of Noah move east to the plain, and now Lot moves east toward Sodom. It should also be noted that Lot's choice moved him away from Canaan, the land that God now gives Abraham.

> Something we're all familiar with around the Christmas season are the wisemen who come "from the east."

Something we're all familiar with around the Christmas season are the wisemen who come "from the east." These are nonbelievers who come seeking Jesus. Another example is found in the wilderness sanctuary, which sat from east to west with the Most Holy Place in the west. Sinners who approached the sanctuary with their offerings and sacrifices come "from the east."

This is not to cast aspersion on anyone who lives in the east or to laud those who live in the west, but it does open our eyes to the details we might otherwise miss as we are reading the Bible. And for me, it points to a God who is very much into order and symbolism as yet another way we may know Him better.

MAKING IT REAL

These chapters are primarily about Abraham and his journey with God. Abraham is asked by God to go where God leads. That's it. No specifics. No definite destination. And Abraham goes. We recognize this as a strong step in faith. It would be many years before Abraham understood all God intended. And he never saw the descendants that would be as numerous as the stars.

Review your life up to this point. In what ways can you see God leading in your life? What is your faith story?

Remember to look heavenward, count the stars, and *be renewed.*

WEEK TWELVE

Angels Rescue Lot

READ **GENESIS 15-18; 19:1-30**

Genesis 17:21 *"But My covenant I will establish with Isaac, whom Sarah shall bear to you at this set time next year."*

RENEW YOUR MIND

The Bible character I most understand is Sarah. Why? Because she's a "fixer." In her mind, she was God's helper. While this sounds good, if you know her story, it isn't. That's why for me it's full confession time: I'm a problem-solver and sometimes that gets me into trouble. Running ahead of God is never a great idea.

God first gave His promise to Abraham in Genesis 12:2-3. The promise is to make him into a great nation. This promise is repeated in Genesis 13:14-16, but God adds something—land. By chapter 15, we read the promise again, but more is added—an heir, a son of his body. Nation. Land. Son.

Now back to Sarah, our problem-solver. She sizes up what God has said—nation, land, son—recognizes she's too old to provide the son, and decides to help. Her help comes in the form of Hagar, who gives Abraham Ishmael. Imagine living in this camp where two women contend over this "son of the promise" that Hagar has produced, but Sarah claims. Everything appears in place: nation, land, son.

Thirteen years pass before Abraham hears the covenant repeated. Imagine his surprise when God adds a new detail: a second son—Sarah's—the *real* son of the promise. Think about this. Abraham, Sarah, Hagar, and Ishmael, key players in this drama, have lived for 13 years with the idea that Ishmael is the promised son. Imagine the mix of surprise, disappointment, disbelief, and confusion this caused. This was a serious turn of events. Or was it?

God's plan *always* was for Abraham and Sarah to have a son. While Abraham and Sarah heard the promise, they lacked the faith to see how it would be accomplished. When Sarah stepped in to help, both of them lost sight of God's plan because they were focused on the one they had created.

As a "fixer," I can relate. I also want to hurry God along by doing what I can to make things go in the direction I'm sure He wants. This story is a good reminder to be patient. Yes, God gives us gifts of discernment, wisdom, and intelligence, but at the same time, if they are not connected to strong faith in God's guidance and His timing, things can suddenly become what you want and not God's desire for your life. Be patient. Trust God to work out His plan. When you do, you will be renewed. ⓑ

> Abraham, Sarah, Hagar, and Ishmael, key players in this drama, have lived for 13 years with the idea that Ishmael is the promised son.

FURTHER READING

Patriarchs and Prophets, pages 136-144, 156-170

The Story of Redemption, pages 75-79

The Bible Story, vol. 1, pages 156-167

Renew YOUR SPIRIT

make new • restore • replenish • reestablish • revive

DIGGING DEEPER

In Genesis 18, Abraham entertains three visitors, strangers until he recognizes it's the Lord Himself. Although one might think their purpose is to visit Abraham, it's Sarah they have come to see. How do we know? Because the first question to Abraham is: "Where is Sarah, your wife?" (Gen. 18:9)

> Instead of "hard," what you see is the word "Wonderful."

The message they have for Abraham is one he has heard before. This time it's repeated, but said where Sarah is listening behind the tent flap. We do not know if she stepped out, but we do know she laughed—quietly, and to herself. Pregnant? Indeed! You can almost see her shaking her head.

The Lord hears and sees the laugh—the small expression of disbelief that still controls Sarah's ability to comprehend such an amazing idea. Then the Lord asks, "Is anything too hard for the Lord?" (v. 14)

The Hebrew word used for "hard" is *pala'* (paw-law). The same word is found in Isaiah 9:6:

"For unto us a Child is born,
 Unto us a Son is given;
 And the government will be upon His shoulder.
 And His name will be called
 Wonderful, Counselor, Mighty God,
 Everlasting Father, Prince of Peace."

Instead of "hard," what you see is the word "Wonderful." When the Lord says, "Is anything too hard for the Lord?" He's not talking about how difficult it is for an old woman to become pregnant. He's referencing that it's "too wonderful," "too amazing," "too marvelous,"—more than words can describe.

And that's who our God is—amazing, awe-inspiring, and more than we can understand. While Sarah's laugh was one of disbelief, it's not why God named their son, "laughter." This baby would be one where Sarah could not contain her joy for her son or the God that cared enough to offer her blessings beyond what she could ever imagine. Too wonderful.

"Is anything too hard for *the Lord?*"

MAKING IT REAL

The same word, *pala'*, used in Genesis 18:14 and Isaiah 9:6, is used in other places of the Bible. Look up some of these verses and contemplate the "wonderfulness" of God. How has He been "too amazing" in your life?

Job 5:9; Job 37:5; Psalm 9:1; Psalm 40:5; Jeremiah 32:7

WEEK THIRTEEN

Abraham and Isaac Trust God

> **READ** **GENESIS 21:1-21; 22:1-19**

Genesis 22:5 And Abraham said to his young men, "Stay here with the donkey; the lad and I will go yonder and worship, and we will come back to you."

> **RENEW YOUR MIND**

The story of Abraham and Isaac is an unusual one. We understand its significance, but we may struggle with the request. Sacrificing your son to God on an altar seems contrary to all we know about God. So what can we learn about God that we have not known previously?

Isaac was the "son of the covenant." We know how important he is as he will be the one who facilitates Abraham's legacy of descendants. To sacrifice him seems counterproductive. Surely, Abraham saw that, yet he moves forward in complete obedience.

We may be able to see what Abraham learns from this test, but does God benefit? He does. Look at verse 12. "And He said, "Do not lay your hand on the lad, or do anything to him; for now I know that you fear God, since you have not withheld your son, your only son, from Me."

I remember one Friday evening settling into the Sabbath, when the door opened and in walked my oldest daughter. She was away at college, and "just because," she traveled the 500-plus miles to surprise me and my husband. While I'm glad I didn't know she was on the road all day, it is something I'll always remember. It was evidence of her love for us.

God already knows what will happen. This "test" of Abraham, in God's eyes, was already accomplished. God knew that Abraham would obey. So why ask? Because knowing that we are loved is different than the actions that evidence it. I already knew my daughter loved me. There was no doubt there. But her decision to drive all day for about 36 hours of family time spoke of her love for us, her family.

God benefited from Abraham's actions. Abraham trusted God. He loved God. He believed in God's promises. But it wasn't just head or heart knowledge, it was active. Abraham's gathering the wood, the fire, the knife, and traveling for three days to a remote location to sacrifice his beloved son showed his "fear" of the Lord. It was active belief, trust, and love.

God loves us just as He loved Abraham. He also knows our hearts. Even though we have accepted His gift of salvation, even if He is the one we worship and adore, we still need to demonstrate our love. Prayer. Praise. Testimony. Intentionally loving God. It's how we are renewed.

> God loves us just as He loved Abraham.

FURTHER READING

Patriarchs and Prophets, pages 145-170

The Story of Redemption, pages 79-83

The Bible Story, vol. 1, pages 168-176

Renew YOUR SPIRIT

make new • restore • replenish • reestablish • revive

DIGGING DEEPER

In Genesis 22:1, the Hebrew word used for God is *Elohim*. If literally translated, it can mean "the God" or even "the gods." This is not typical for the author of Genesis. Normally one sees the name *Yahweh* or *El Shaddai*. One possible explanation is that the reader needs to look back to the last name of God used to identify which God is speaking. Thus, the reader reads, "the God," and asks, "which God?"

> This God is one that offers constancy, stability, and security.

We don't have to go back far to find out. Genesis 21:33 reveals which God. Abraham "called on the name of the Lord, the Everlasting God." The Hebrew word here can also mean "perpetual," "evermore," or "always." This God is one that offers constancy, stability, and security.

If we review where Abraham had been prior to the beginning of Genesis 22, it fits. He's faced the difficult situation with Hagar and Ishmael, the destruction of Sodom, the arrival of another son, and the settling into Beersheba. After years of turmoil, unrest, and challenges, Abraham can rest. Isaac is maturing into a fine son, Sarah is happy, and all is well. The "God of Always" is fully present.

Of course, after Gen. 22:1, comes the test—one that undoes everything. Just as Abraham thought he could sit back and relax; he's faced with the most difficult circumstance yet. But experience with the Everlasting God, the Perpetual God, the Enduring God, gives him peace and courage to obey.

When all is finished and the ram in the thicket has been sacrificed in Isaac's place, Abraham calls the place, "The Lord will Provide." How fitting. The "Everlasting God" is also the "God who delivers."

MAKING IT REAL

What kind of test might God ask of you that would be difficult? Think about the reasons it might be painful to obey. What scriptures can you find that would help make surrendering easier?

Even though we have *accepted His gift,* we still need to demonstrate our love.

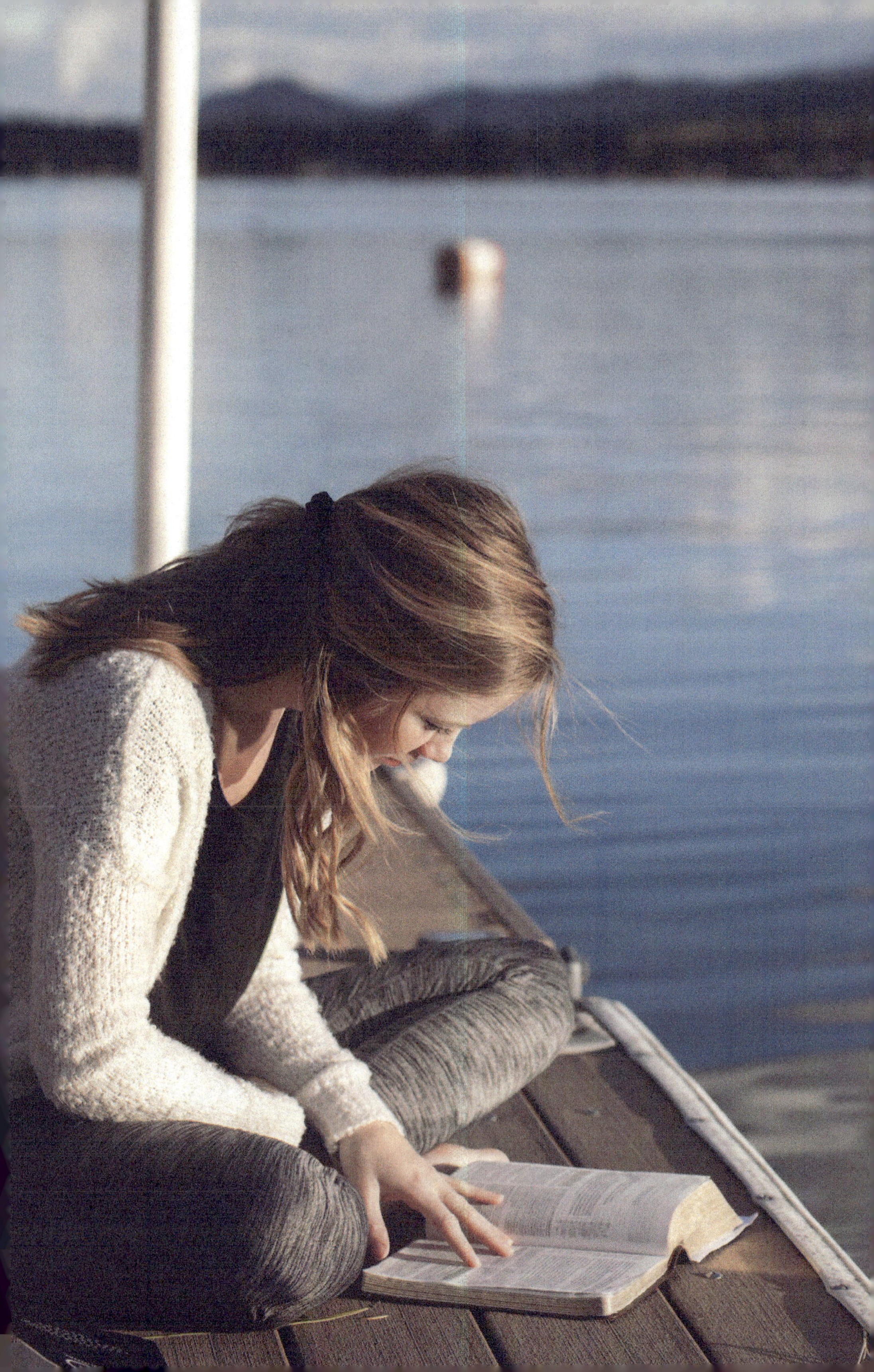

PART TWO

Learning His Love

WEEK FOURTEEN

A Bride for Isaac

READ **GENESIS 24**

Genesis 24:57-58 So they said, "We will call the young woman and ask her personally." Then they called Rebekah and said to her, "Will you go with this man?" And she said, "I will go."

RENEW YOUR MIND

The denomination that I work for has developed a strategic plan called "I Will Go." This plan is focused primarily on answering God's call to witness to unreached people around the world. "I Will Go" stirs your heart to think of missionaries in foreign lands; of people accepting the gospel in what was once a place of darkness. After reading and studying Genesis 24, I realized it is something much more meaningful.

Consider the story. Abraham desires a wife for his beloved son. He does not want Isaac to leave the land of promise and so entrusts a servant to seek a wife from his family. The servant travels about 900 miles with a caravan of 10 camels laden with gifts. Upon arrival he prays that God points out the right girl by her offer to water his camels. Before the prayer is finished, Rebekah arrives and all unfolds just as the servant requested.

Knowing now exactly who God selected for Isaac, the servant is anxious to be on his way to deliver to his master's son this valuable gift of the perfect bride. The family, wanting her to stay a little longer, asks Rebekah if she's willing to leave, having only known for 24 hours that she is to become the bride of a perfect stranger. Her response is short and to the point: "I will go."

Think of all that is encompassed in her response. In this case, she isn't an evangelist, a missionary, or even a witness. She is simply accepting God's call. A man she does not know arrives bearing gifts and the request to marry a man she also does not know. She must leave her family going to a distant country, probably never seeing her home again. Yet she does not hesitate. "I will go." Like Abraham, she also takes a step of faith into an unknown future.

God calls us each and every day to follow Him. Sometimes it is to unseen places to do unknown things. But He continually supplies us with the strength and grace to do whatever is asked. Our simple response should be "I will go." It is expressing our faith day by day in the One who calls us where we find renewal. ®

> **She must leave her family going to a distant country, probably never seeing her home again. Yet she does not hesitate. "I will go."**

FURTHER READING

Patriarchs and Prophets, pages 171-176

The Story of Redemption, pages 84-86

The Bible Story, vol. 1, pages 177-186

Renew YOUR SPIRIT

make new • restore • replenish • reestablish • revive

DIGGING DEEPER

The coming together of Isaac and Rebekah can read like a sweet romance—the beautiful bride from a distant land who meets the young groom who loves her and makes her his wife. But their story is rich with symbolism related to Jesus and His bride, the church.

> The story of Isaac and Rebekah can read like a sweet romance, but it's also rich with symbolism related to Jesus and His bride, the church.

Both Rebekah and the Church:*
- Were chosen for marriage before they knew it (Eph. 1:3-4)
- Were necessary for the accomplishment of God's eternal purpose (Eph. 3:10-11)
- Were destined to share in the glory of the son (Son) (John 17:22-23)
- Learned of the son (Son) through his representative
- Must leave all with joy to be with the son (Son)
- Were loved and cared for by the son (Son)

Both Isaac and Jesus:
- Were promised before their coming
- Finally appeared at the appointed time
- Were conceived and born miraculously
- Were given a special name before birth
- Were offered up in sacrifice by the father
- Were brought back from the dead (symbolically for Isaac)
- Were head of a great company to bless all people
- Prepared a place for their bride
- Had a ministry of prayer until united with the bride

*Original thoughts from David Guzik, enduringword.com

God calls us
each and every day
to follow Him.

I will go.

MAKING IT REAL

When my girls were toddlers, I began praying specifically for their husbands. I knew that somewhere God had little boys who would eventually grow up to become the one who would love and treasure my daughters. I prayed for them and for their parents that they would grow into fine Christian young men.

As my girls grew and became young women who would begin dating, my prayers changed a bit. Now I asked God not only to continue to care for those young men, but to open the eyes and hearts of my girls to only the one God wanted for them. I can say with gratitude that my prayers were answered. Both my sons-in-law are answers to my prayers; both girls are happy, loved, and cherished. My heart is full and I am abundantly grateful to God for creating two new Christian households where His name is praised.

Do you have children or grandchildren, nieces, or nephews? Pray for them as Abraham and Eliezer did for Isaac. It's never too early or late to start. Pray for them to discover the Christian man or woman that is their hearts desire, but more importantly the one that God has designed just for them.

WEEK FIFTEEN

Twins that Weren't Alike

> **READ** **GENESIS 25:7-11, 19-34; 27:1-40**

Genesis 25:32 *And Esau said, "Look, I am about to die; so what is this birthright to me?"*

> **RENEW YOUR MIND**

As I write, I have at least two job opportunities open to me. Mind you, they aren't genuine offers, but I'm aware of their potential. The temptation to begin thinking whether either is something I want to do with my life before they even materialize is great. In fact, I could perhaps think of ways to make them more probable.

This is a bit like Rebekah and Jacob in our story. We tend to focus on Jacob. He is, after all, the one who will move on in the story. But to do so is to miss the important lesson that comes from all involved—a lesson in patience, or rather the lack of it.

- Rebekah is told the future of her twins before they are even born. Like Mary, she ponders this in her heart. Like Sarah, she decides to help God.
- Esau returns from a great adventure famished. He arrives just as Jacob is cooking a delectable pot of red lentils. The aroma drives Esau to such distraction that he cannot wait. His desire for food causes him to make a foolish decision.
- Jacob desires the spiritual leadership of the family. Jacob doesn't actually have an experiential relationship with God, but he wants all that goes with it. When an opportunity presents itself to take it from Esau, he can't wait.
- Isaac also understands the prophecy, recognizes Esau's lack of spiritual qualifications, but also knows Rebekah and Jacob desire its fulfillment to be in Jacob. Esau, however, is his favorite, and well, Isaac can't wait.

See the pattern? Impatience. It can get the best of us, causing us to run ahead of God. We see what appears to be a family with confused priorities, favoritism, and deceit and we shake our heads. What we really should be doing is recognizing that they are us. If truthful, we will admit to also being impatient. The instant gratification of today's society has trained us to want immediate responses. This desire may get us what we want, but it can leave God out of the equation.

Although we may be tempted to race ahead to do or plan something we might think is best, allow God to work. It may take longer than we want, but if we accept each day as a gift, doing what God wants us to do for that day, it is enough. Wait on God and be renewed. Ⓡ

> Impatience can get the best of us, causing us to run ahead.

FURTHER READING

Patriarchs and Prophets, pages 177-182

The Story of Redemption, pages 87-89

The Bible Story, vol. 2, pages 9-19

Renew YOUR SPIRIT

make new • restore • replenish • reestablish • revive

DIGGING DEEPER

The idea of a birthright may be something we have trouble understanding. In Old Testament times, the birthright belonged to the eldest son. It involved the inheritance of the family wealth, but more importantly it was the passing of the priesthood from the father to the son. To receive the birthright was a tremendous responsibility and one that should be cherished.

> Will we serve God or the world? To choose God is to acknowledge our spiritual birthright.

Today we may understand inheritance better. Someone bequeaths their earthly possessions and bank accounts to us. We do, however, still have a spiritual birthright. It first is expressed through our parents, primarily the mother, to the children. The mother's attitude toward the child, her level of love, grace, and blessing that she shares along with the teaching of spiritual truth bequeaths an immeasurable wealth. But it does not end there.

As adults we choose every day whom we will serve—will we serve God or the world? To choose God is to acknowledge our spiritual birthright. To focus primarily on what the world gives is to spurn the blessing God has in store for us.

"Esau lusted for a favorite dish, and sacrificed his birthright to gratify appetite. After his lustful appetite had been gratified he saw his folly, but found no space for repentance though he sought it carefully and with tears. There are very many who are like Esau. *He represents a class who have a special, valuable blessing within their reach,—the immortal inheritance, life that is as enduring as the life of God, the Creator of the universe, happiness immeasurable, and an eternal weight of glory,—but who have so long indulged their appetites, passions, and inclinations, that their power to discern and appreciate the value of eternal things is weakened*" (*Testimonies to the Church*, vol. 2, p. 38, emphasis supplied).

Never let it be said that you are "selling your birthright for a mess of pottage" (*Testimonies to the Church*, vol. 2, p. 37).

Perhaps Hebrews 12:16 says it best: "Watch out for the Esau syndrome: trading away God's lifelong gift in order to satisfy a short-term appetite" (*The Message*).

Although we may be tempted to race ahead, *allow God to work.*

MAKING IT REAL

Isaac tested Jacob using his senses. He used logic (why was Esau back so soon?), touch (apparently goat hair passed the test), hearing (the one test Jacob failed), taste (goat that tasted like venison), and smell (the final test). Make a list of how you experience God using your five senses: sight, sound, taste, smell, and touch.

WEEK SIXTEEN

Jacob's New Name

READ **GENESIS 27:41-46, 28-32**

Genesis 32:1, 2 *So Jacob went on his way, and the angels of God met him. When Jacob saw them, he said, "This is God's camp." And he called the name of that place Mahanaim.*

RENEW YOUR MIND

Believe it or not, I'm writing this devotional from the passenger seat of our car. I'm not a fan of long distance trips involving *any* form of transportation, but I have discovered several coping mechanisms to make things easier, such as what I'm doing now—working on my computer as a distraction from the traffic around me. Another is angels.

For as long as I can remember, when a situation causes me to be anxious or afraid, I visualize being surrounded by angels. They surround my house like an army. They fly above, below, in front, and on each wing of an airplane. They clear the traffic from around the car. I could go on.

In this week's lesson we encounter the familiar story of Jacob wrestling with an Angel. We will return to this in a moment, but first I want to draw your attention to another angel sighting earlier in the story.

As Laban leaves and Jacob continued his journey, he is met by "angels of God" (Gen. 32:1). The Bible doesn't reveal what happened at this meeting, how many angels there were, or why they were sent. But it's significant enough for Jacob to name the place of meeting "Mahanaim," which means "double camp." What Jacob saw was exactly what my mind imagines—his family completely encircled by angels.

Jacob isn't comforted long by this angel revelation. His distress, heightened by the news of Esau's imminent arrival, caused him to fall back on his own resourcefulness. He separated his family into two camps. He sent an amazing number of animals in separate entourages to placate the angry Esau. Finally, he sent his family across the Jabbok River, leaving himself alone, no less distressed than before. Then, and only then, did he realize his great need of God.

I think we sometimes identify more with the wrestling than we do with trust. We hit a crisis in our life, flee to God, and then wrestle with Him through our anger, frustration, or grief. But we forget about the "double camp," the band of angels that surrounds us every moment of every day. While Jacob emerged changed because of his face-to-face encounter with God, it did not mean God wasn't there before. Jacob simply lacked the trust to believe.

Don't wait for a crisis to meet God. Yes, you will have your nights of wrestling. But each day, take a moment to visualize His presence. Open your eyes in faith and be renewed. ⓫

> **While Jacob emerged changed because of his face-to-face encounter with God, it did not mean God wasn't there for him before.**

FURTHER READING

Patriarchs and Prophets, pages 183-198

The Story of Redemption, pages 89-96

The Bible Story, vol. 2, pages 20-35

Renew YOUR SPIRIT

make new • restore • replenish • reestablish • revive

DIGGING DEEPER

Note that scripture does not say Jacob wrestles with the Angel, but "a man wrestled with him" (verse 24). At first Jacob believed Esau or an enemy had surprised him, and he struggled for his life. Interestingly, the assailant (who we later learn was Jesus) and Jacob appeared evenly matched. It's only when Jacob's hip was touched and put out of joint that recognition dawned as to the identity of the Man. Jacob was not dissuaded by the pain but continued to tenaciously hold on, recognizing that God was his only answer. Gone was the conniving, clever, deceiver, replaced by a weeping and contrite Jacob pleading for a blessing.

> Jacob was not dissuaded by the pain but continued to tenaciously hold on, recognizing that God was his only answer.

The last time Jacob received a blessing it was through disguise and deceit. This time he came open and ready to receive what God intended for him. Blessing received, Jacob, now forever known as Israel, went forward in full reliance of faith and trust in God. The wrestling match began as a contest to win, but Jacob became a conqueror only when he was weakest, not when he relied solely on his own abilities and resources.

MAKING IT REAL

Sometimes God needs to get us alone before He can get our attention. Only when Jacob had sent his family across the river and was alone did God approach. How can you find alone time to spend time with God away from the noise and distractions of a busy life?

Don't wait for a crisis
to meet God.

WEEK SEVENTEEN

Family Problems

READ **GENESIS 33, 35, 37, 39, 40**

Genesis 39:9 *"There is no one greater in this house than I, nor has he kept back anything from me but you, because you are his wife. How then can I do this great wickedness, and sin against God?"*

RENEW YOUR MIND

One of the saddest verses in the Bible is Genesis 40:23: "Yet the chief butler did not remember Joseph, but forgot him." Chapter 41 then begins: "Then it came to pass, at the end of two full years . . ." Joseph spent 13 years of his life as a slave or a prisoner. How much of this time was in Potiphar's house versus prison is not revealed, but we can understand after interpreting the dream correctly for the cupbearer, his high hopes of being released. You can imagine his disappointment. Waiting day after day, then weeks, then months. Nothing.

A story has made its way around the internet told in different ways, but with the same message. One version goes like this:

A woman had been a longtime missionary to Africa. She had become a part of the community and they loved her as one of their own. The day came when she decided to return home. The villagers gave her a farewell party. One of her students presented her with a gift poorly wrapped in brown paper. Opening it, she saw a seashell, seemingly unremarkable in its appearance, yet the woman recognized it as one that was only found on a beach some 30 miles away from where they lived.

"Where did you get this?" she asked.

"I walked to the beach to find it for you," he replied.

"Walked?" she gasped.

He smiled. "Teacher, the journey is part of the gift!"

When we look at Joseph's life in its entirety, we know it ends well. We might even accept that in spite of the challenges this teenager might have needed to experience a few hard lessons before becoming a leader of the greatest nation at that time. Joseph, however, would not know the ending while he was living his life. Being a slave wasn't great. Being a prisoner was worse. But one thing we do know—Joseph had not forgotten God (Gen. 39:9). He had somehow found contentment in his journey despite the disappointments. The journey was part of the gift.

So where are you in your journey? Sitting amid piles of never-ending laundry? Working in a job that lacks affirmation or challenges? Close to retirement and feeling unaccomplished? Everyone isn't Joseph. It's quite possible your journey won't end in an exciting promotion or amazing achievement. You may simply be living an ordinary life. What *is* important is finding contentment in your journey. But what about the gift?

God's done that for you already! The first gift was giving His Son, Jesus, so that your life can forever be saved in Him. The second gift is coming. While your journey today may seem mundane, there is a reward at the end. Jesus is preparing a place for you all while you face the cares and challenges each day brings. The journey is part of the gift. Be content. Look up. Find joy in your journey. Jesus is coming soon!

> He had somehow found contentment in his journey despite the disappointments. The journey was part of the gift.

FURTHER READING

Patriarchs and Prophets, pages 198-219

The Story of Redemption, pages 96-103

The Bible Story, vol. 2, pages 36-56

Renew YOUR SPIRIT

make new • restore • replenish • reestablish • revive

DIGGING DEEPER

Several observations as we finish the Genesis story.

> **How will God deliver all He has promised?**

- God made a covenant with Abraham. In it, He promised him land as well as more descendants than the stars.
- Isaac is the promised heir to Abraham, but it begs the question as to how one son can possibly provide the legacy God has promised. Perhaps Abraham wonders this as well.
- Favoritism creeps into the story as the twin sons of Isaac and Rebekah are born. The covenant appears to be in danger as we read about Esau, the careless and cavalier firstborn. His brother Jacob, the deceiver, saves the day, but stealing the birthright doesn't seem to be what God had in mind.
- We get a better idea of how Abraham's seed might populate the earth as we read of son after son being born to Jacob, even though it involves four women in the process! The covenant, so important in the beginning, while definitely more promising as we count Abraham's descendants, seems to be lacking as it relates to the land, because Jacob no longer lives in Canaan.
- God tells Jacob to move back to Canaan and the story seems to right itself again. Jacob and Esau patch things up; Isaac is reunited with Jacob; Jacob's 12 sons grow to manhood.
- Favoritism raises its ugly head once again as it is repeated in Jacob's household. Jacob prizes Joseph, oldest son of Rachel, so much so that Joseph becomes a challenge to his increasingly unsavory brothers. The selling of Joseph to traders, his relocation to Egypt, and the deception that Jacob's sons now play on their father, does not seem to bode well for God's purpose. How will God deliver all He has promised to Abraham with this dysfunctional family?
- Finally, next week we will learn that Jacob's entire family, the family of the promise, will move to Egypt once again away from the land of the covenant. There they will remain for 400 years. While we may wonder how God will bring about resolution, we know that He has led them there purposely. Joseph's slavery has become Israel's salvation at least for now.

The *journey* is part of the gift.

MAKING IT REAL

Our story revealed that the journey is part of the gift. Take time to reflect on your journey. You can do this in several ways depending on your time:

1. **Lots of time:** Get a piece of paper. Make two columns. In one column list the highlights of your life thus far. In the other column, list any events or incidences that were challenging. Then map your journey, identifying the highs and lows along the way. Mark on your map where you saw or felt God in your journey.
2. **Some time:** Get a piece of paper. Make three columns. In one column list the highlights of your life thus far. In the second, list those times where you were challenged. In the third column detail where you saw or felt God working in your life. Can you see where God was leading even when it was through difficulties?
3. **Multi-tasking:** If you only have time when doing something else (folding laundry, doing dishes, feeding a baby), think about three times in your life that were super highs. Then think of any times that were challenging. How can you praise God for both the highs and lows? Talk with Him about your journey while you multi-task.
4. **Too busy to stop:** It's OK! We all have times in our life like this. God understands. This is when you praise Him for being with you on your journey. Take a deep breath. Exhale slowly. Repeat: "I can do all things through Christ who strengthens me" (Phil. 4:13).

WEEK EIGHTEEN

Faithfulness Rewarded

READ **GENESIS 41-50**

Genesis 45:5,7 *"But now, do not therefore be grieved or angry with yourselves because you sold me here; for God sent me before you to preserve life. And God sent me before you to preserve a prosperity for you in the earth, and to save your lives by a great deliverance."*

RENEW YOUR MIND

I like chocolate. Put some nuts in the chocolate and I like it even better. If those nuts are hazelnuts or almonds, we're talking serious temptation. Resisting chocolate for me is generally under control from February to November. But when December rolls around, candy seems to become abundant, and I've discovered that it takes about the month of January to empty our pantry of all things tempting that arrived during the holidays. And then it begins. Teaching my body yet again that chocolate needs to be in moderation or not at all to be healthy and thin(ner).

While this probably isn't the best example of character building I could offer you, it is exactly what I thought of today as we reach the conclusion of Joseph's story. This was no ordinary man. As we review his life, from riches to rags to riches again, everything he did whether son, slave, prisoner, or potentate seemed to emulate a strong character. How did he consistently stay secure in the presence of temptation?

Answer: Joseph never let go of God. Even when it seemed to Joseph that God let go of him, Joseph clung to God. We see glimpses of this in his response to Potiphar's wife (Gen. 39:9) as well as in his response to his brothers (Gen. 45:5-8). Joseph determined that he would follow God in any and all circumstances—no matter how small, difficult, or distasteful. For Joseph, wherever he was was where God wanted him to be. While temptation was present, it did not conquer him but instead built character.

"There are few who realize the influence of the little things of life upon the development of character. Nothing with which we have to do is really small. The varied circumstances that we meet day by day are designed to test our faithfulness and to qualify us for greater trusts. . . . By faithfulness in that which is least they [people who follow God] acquire strength to be faithful in greater matters" (*Patriarchs and Prophets*, p. 222-223).

That chocolate bar in my pantry completely qualifies as a little thing. But resisting it or at least parsing it out over days instead of consuming it in minutes, helps build my character. The irritations of life—work, people, traffic, or whatever is eating away at you or causing serious temptation—may seem big or small, but they become tests for us to choose between God and His plan or our own way.

Sometimes we will fail. Sometimes we win. But keeping score isn't what it's all about. Having Jesus in focus is what matters. Character to fit us for heaven is something that happens over a lifetime. With every decision involving Him, knowing we are right where He needs us to be, we will find ourselves building character one moment at a time, even when it's as small as resisting chocolate.

> **Sometimes we will fail. Sometimes we win. But keeping score isn't what it's all about.**

FURTHER READING

Patriarchs and Prophets, pages 219-240

The Story of Redemption, pages 103, 104

The Bible Story, vol. 2, pages 57-72

Renew YOUR SPIRIT

make new • restore • replenish • reestablish • revive

DIGGING DEEPER

To read about Joseph and desire to emulate him isn't a bad thing—in fact, what you may not realize is that the life of Joseph is parallel to Christ's. To make choices as Joseph did is another way to say, I want to live like Jesus. Consider these comparisons between the two:

> To make choices as Joseph did is another way to say, I want to live like Jesus.

JOSEPH	JESUS
Jealousy caused Joseph's brothers to sell him into slavery	Jealousy caused the priests to have Jesus arrested, ultimately having Him killed
Joseph became second to Pharaoh at age 30	Jesus began His ministry at 30
Joseph, by being in Egypt, became a savior to his family	Jesus, through His crucifixion, was the Redeemer of all mankind
Joseph was sold by his brothers	Jesus was sold by one of His disciples
Joseph was falsely accused and thrown into prison even though he was innocent	Jesus was falsely accused and treated like a prisoner although He was innocent
Joseph was patient in spite of injustice	Jesus did not complain and was silent in the presence of injustice
Joseph was unrecognized by his brothers when they came to Egypt	Jesus was unrecognized as the Messiah when He came to earth
Joseph forgave his brothers	Jesus forgave those who abused and killed Him, but also offers forgiveness to all who seek Him as their Savior.

We are *right* where He *needs us* to be.

MAKING IT REAL

Joseph was given the daughter of the priest of On as his wife. Together they had two sons. Joseph's sons grew up as the grandsons of one of the most high-profile priest families in Egypt. Their father was second to Pharaoh in his power. Yet at the end of Jacob's life, Joseph brought his two sons to be blessed by his father, a shepherd, and of no consequence in the eyes of Egyptians. This blessing was not simply a rite of passage, but it was a joining of his sons to his father's family leaving behind the riches, glories, and temptations that a life in Egypt would offer.

Your children are the most precious gifts that God has given to you. We are told to daily bind our children upon the altar of the Lord (*Child Guidance*, p. 527). We are asked to be ready to answer the question at the judgment: What have you done with My little flock that I entrusted to you? (Manuscript 70, 1903). These are serious and sobering questions.

Whether there are children in the home or you're living in an empty nest or you've never had children, Joseph's choice for his sons should give us pause. It's never too late to find time for spiritual moments with children or with those around us. Plan today to look for ways to connect with others in spiritual ways.

WEEK NINETEEN

God Prepares a Deliverer

READ **EXODUS 1-6**

Exodus 2:3 But when she could no longer hide him, she took an ark of bulrushes for him, daubed it with asphalt and pitch, put the child in it, and laid it in the reeds by the river's bank.

RENEW YOUR MIND

Perhaps you've heard the story of the boy who had his hand stuck in a vase. Wanting to free the boy without breaking the vase posed a problem. Various attempts failed until it was discovered that the boy was holding a penny in his fist. Not wanting to lose his precious find, he held on tightly. Only after much coaxing did he open his hand dropping the penny. Of course, not only did he have his freedom, but upending the vase, the penny as well.

Jochebed teaches a similar lesson. I'm fairly certain that the last thing she wanted to do was leave her 3-month-old floating on the Nile River. But her faith allowed her to let go of her son. In so doing, God gave him back, and only in a matter of hours. What do we hold tightly in our hearts or our hands that if we let go, God would be allowed to bless us in more ways than we can imagine?

* * *

I once had a job where I was successful. There was only one problem. I was bored. I set my eyes on another job that appeared more interesting. When the opportunity presented itself, I went for it. It was a mistake, and a hard lesson—one that lingers with me even today. Moses, seeing injustice, decided to put himself in the position of deliverer—one Egyptian at a time. He decided to do things his way instead of God's. Jumping ahead or rewriting God's plan can place us in circumstances God never intended. Waiting on God may be hard to do, but a lesson, like Moses, we must learn.

*　*　*

Moses, shoeless and troubled, kneels in front of the burning bush begging that someone else serve as the deliverer. God then asks: "What is in your hand?" For Moses, it was a shepherd's rod. Nothing special, but it became the tool he would use to free a nation. The same question echoes down the millennia. What is in your hand? What has God given you that can be used for His kingdom? Only an individual can answer such a personal question, but the response, when used with and for God, can become the means of serving in mighty and miraculous ways.

Letting go. Letting God. Serving Him. In these we are renewed.

What do we hold tightly in our hearts or our hands that if we let go, God would be allowed to bless?

FURTHER READING

Patriarchs and Prophets, pages 241-263

The Story of Redemption, pages 105-116

The Bible Story, vol. 2, pages 75-105

Renew YOUR SPIRIT

make new • restore • replenish • reestablish • revive

DIGGING DEEPER

My daughter has been teaching English in one of our Adventist schools. She taught a unit on "Identity" using various methods as a way to allow the teenagers in her classroom to explore the answer to the question: Who am I? While it seems a simple question, for them it proved to be challenging.

> Moses could certainly be forgiven if he had an identity crisis.

Moses could certainly be forgiven if he had an identity crisis. He was raised by his mother for 12 years (Ellen White, *Patriarchs and Prophets*, p. 244). An additional 38 years was spent being raised by his adopted mother in the palaces of Egypt. Compare for a moment what that might have meant in his environment, food, clothing, entertainment, and faith. The riches of the most powerful country in the world contrasted with the slave's cabin and lifestyle.

But look what happens when Moses goes on a walkabout in Egypt (Ex. 3:11). The Bible says he went out to "see his brethren and looked at their burdens." He saw an Egyptian beating an Israelite (v. 11), again "one of his brethren." Moses seems clear on who he is—he's an Israelite. He identifies with God's people. Further reading in Hebrews affirms this:

"By faith Moses, when he became of age, refused to be called the son of Pharaoh's daughter, choosing rather to suffer affliction with the people of God than to enjoy the passing pleasures of sin, esteeming the reproach of Christ greater riches than the treasures in Egypt; for he looked to the reward" (Hebrews 11:24-26).

It went a little deeper than identity for Moses. Acts 7:23-25 reveals even more about this story: "Now when he was forty years old, it came into his heart to visit his brethren, the children of Israel. And seeing one of them suffer wrong, he defended and avenged him who was oppressed, and struck down the Egyptian. For he supposed that his brethren would have understood that God would deliver them by his hand, but they did not understand."

Recognizing oneself as a child of God is only half of the equation. Accepting His will and desire for our lives, in His way, with His timing, is how we arrive at contentment.

What has *God given you* that can be used for His kingdom?

MAKING IT REAL

The early life of Moses has much for us to contemplate. Consider these questions:
1. As a parent, in what ways **can you give your child back to God** each day?
2. If you had to answer the question, **Who am I?**, what would be your response?
3. What things, talents, or blessings are **"in your hand"** that can be used by God today?

WEEK TWENTY

God Shows His Power

READ **EXODUS 7:1-12:33**

Exodus 7:3 "And I will harden Pharaoh's heart, and multiply My signs and My wonders in the land of Egypt."

RENEW YOUR MIND

One of Vincent Van Gogh's most popular works, "Café Terrace at Night," at first glance seems to be exactly what its title describes. But if one lingers and studies the painting, it reveals something about the artist. In 1888, Van Gogh was contemplating life, including he said, "[the] tremendous need for, shall I say the word—for religion."

The painting is a French café, but a closer look reveals the diners arranged similarly to the painting of DaVinci's "The Last Supper." There is the distinct shape of Jesus as the Server and the disciples sitting at the tables, with even the suggestion of a disappearing Judas. Van Gogh painted not just what he saw, but what he felt.

The story of the plagues in Exodus is a bit like that painting. It can simply be a story of pestilence sent by God. But to continue on without lingering for a closer look will cause us to miss important revelations about God.

The first hint is the word used to describe the waters of the Nile being changed to blood (Ex. 7:19). It is the same Hebrew word used to describe the creation of the sea (Genesis 1:10). Creation began with light, air, sea, and land. To this God added vegetation, creatures in the sea, in air, and on land. Finally, it culminated in the creation of man.

The plagues closely resemble an undoing of Creation. Instead of the order God brought into chaos, God brought chaos to the order in Egypt. Frogs came from the *sea*, lice from the *earth*, and flies from the *air*. Pestilence attacks *animals* with disease and boils; hail and locust completely destroyed the *vegetation*. Darkness obliterated the *light*. Finally, *man* himself was undone in the death of the firstborn.[1] Not only did God win the war against Egyptian gods, but He established Himself as the Creator. What God spoke into existence in the beginning, He can also undo.

Certainly, Pharaoh came up against a God like no other he had ever encountered. But this show of Creation power wasn't only for him or for the Egyptians. It was also for the Israelites. Many of them were comfortable in Egypt, so much so they didn't want to leave. There was nothing in Moses' revelation of God as Redeemer (Ex. 6:6) that excited them. While one fell blow could have accomplished their freedom, God showed His power 10 times so reluctant Israel would choose to leave. There would be no hesitation in their response to His justice, power, and love.[2]

It sounds odd that someone living the life of a slave wouldn't long for freedom, yet we too live the life of a slave—slaves to sin. Jesus came to break the bonds of slavery, to free us from sin, to lead us to freedom. We struggle here on earth, with chains that bind, not recognizing that the Creator and Redeemer has already delivered us with that same justice, love, and power. Look up. Embrace freedom. Be renewed.

> The plagues closely resemble an undoing of Creation.

FURTHER READING

Patriarchs and Prophets, pages 263-280

The Story of Redemption, pages 116-119

The Bible Story, vol. 2, pages 106-120

---

[1] An article by Ziony Zevit, printed in *Bible Review*, June 1990, and reprinted in *Bible History Daily*, July 2011, describes this interpretation in depth.

[2] Read more in *Patriarchs and Prophets*, p. 260.

Renew YOUR SPIRIT

make new • restore • replenish • reestablish • revive

DIGGING DEEPER

While the plagues demonstrated a reversing of Creation, they were also a direct attack against the gods of Egypt, aiming directly at Egyptian belief and culture (Num. 33:4). The plagues not only declared God as the most powerful to the Egyptians, but to Israel as well, some of whom worshiped alongside the Egyptians.

> The plagues were also a direct attack against the gods of Egypt, aiming directly at Egyptian belief and culture.

While not all of the plagues humiliated a god or goddess, they did demonstrate the complete lack of power in wood and stone. Each plague moved up the hierarchy until the most powerful Egyptian gods, Re and Osiris, were defeated. Consider the following:

First plague	Blood	Against the god **Khnum**, creator of water and life; or **Hapi**, the Nile god; or **Osiris**, whose bloodstream was the Nile
Second plague	Frogs	**Heket**, a goddess of childbirth
Fifth plague	Cattle	**Hathor**, the mother and sky goddess was represented as a cow; or **Apis**, symbol of fertility represented as a bull
Seventh plague	Hail	Against **Seth**, who manifested himself in wind and storms; and/or **Isis**, goddess of life, who grinds, spun flax, and wove cloth; or **Min**, who was worshiped as a god of fertility and vegetation as well as the protector of crops
Eighth plague	Locusts	
Ninth plague	Darkness	**Amon-Re, Aten, Atum**, or **Horus**, deities associated with the sun
Tenth plague	Death of firstborn	**Osiris**, the judge of the dead and patron saint of Pharaoh

He has already delivered us.
Embrace freedom.

MAKING IT REAL

Ever feel like a slave? It's OK. Go ahead and admit it. We've all been there. We're cleaning, trying to stay ahead of clutter, doing laundry, shopping, planning meals, working, volunteering, and often it is without thanks or affirmation. What's crazy is that we can actually get comfortable in all the busyness even if it isn't rewarding at times. What God did for Israel was shake them up by revealing His power—power that was released to free them.

   That same power is offered to you. Sometimes God does shake us up in ways that are uncomfortable so that we can recognize our need for freedom. Think about it this week. How are you a slave? What ways is God trying to gain your attention?

WEEK TWENTY-ONE

Free at Last

READ **EXODUS 12:34-42, 50, 51; 13:17-15:21**

Exodus 14:14 *"The Lord will fight for you, and you shall hold your peace."*

RENEW YOUR MIND

Jesus and the disciples were on the Sea of Galilee when a storm arose. Thunder rolled, lightning cut the sky, and the waves pounded the boat. They fought the storm, but their efforts were in vain. Panic set in.

* * *

After the Mt. Carmel experience, Elijah ran before Ahab's chariot in the pouring rain. When he arrives at the city he is confronted by the threat of an angry queen. Panic sends him running again.

* * *

The Israelites left Egypt under the banner of a powerful God who freed them from bondage. They follow the Cloud to the Red Sea. Then another cloud arose—this one of dust. The ground shook with the pounding of horse hooves. The Egyptian army is headed right for them. And they panic.

* * *

Overreaction? Not really. When one experiences what seems to be imminent death from drowning or murder or attack, panic would seem a predictable response. It's what happens next that makes the difference. The disciples turned to Jesus. Elijah turned to God. The Israelites turned *on* Moses and God. Why the difference?

Practiced faith. One does not simply arrive at being a confident Christian. It takes time to develop a relationship with God, to have complete and full belief in

Him, and an experience that assures one of His power and love. It shouldn't be, but sin causes it to be so.

The Israelites were unpracticed. Although they had recently experienced one of the most amazing displays of God's power on their behalf, when fear overtook them their instinct wasn't to go to God or even to Moses. It was to return to where they came as irrational as that seems. Their panic took over and their courage vanished. When God is not a constant, our vision becomes blurred.

Read Exodus 14:13 again as Moses responds to the Israelites. It is good counsel: Don't be afraid. Stand still and watch God work. What you fear will be gone. But don't stop reading. Read verse 14. He adds: The Lord will fight for you. Hold your peace. But do you know what the Hebrew actually says? An accurate and polite translation is: "Be quiet!" A closer read and more to the point is: "Shut up!"

Really? Meek, mild, never-lose-it Moses says, "Shut up!"? Think of it as one of those television/movie moments when a hysterical person is slapped to get their attention. This is a verbal equivalent. Stop the hysteria. Stop the panic. Remember God. Remember the plagues. Look at the Cloud. He has a way out.

Practice faith each day. Rehearse what God has done. Repeat His promises. For when fear threatens, running to God is the answer. Only He can provide a way to bring calm to your storm. Rest in Him each day and be renewed. ⓑ

The disciples turned to Jesus. Elijah turned to God. The Israelites turned *on* Moses and God. Why the difference?

FURTHER READING

Patriarchs and Prophets, pages 281-290

The Story of Redemption, pages 119-125

The Bible Story, vol. 2, pages 121-138

Renew YOUR SPIRIT

make new • restore • replenish • reestablish • revive

DIGGING DEEPER

Have you ever wished for a Cloud? Note the use of the capital C. Not the white puffy kind floating in the sky, but the pillar kind Israel had in the wilderness. I often wish I had this visible Presence to show me I was on the right path, to shelter in its shade, and feel the power emanating from it.

> God steps in, like He did in the time of the exodus. He offers protection.

If you've thought the same, take comfort! Here is a verse I discovered in my study of this Bible story found in Isaiah 4:5.

"Then the Lord will create above every dwelling place of Mount Zion, and above her assemblies, a cloud and smoke by day and the shining of a flaming fire by night. For over all the glory there will be a covering." (NKJV)

Now read the same verse in *The Message*:*

"Then God will bring back the ancient pillar of cloud by day and the pillar of fire by night and mark Mount Zion and everyone in it with his glorious presence, his immense, protective presence, shade from the burning sun and shelter from the driving rain." (Isaiah 4:5)

Do you find yourself exhaling? There is nothing to fear. There is no concern as to what will happen next. We may live in a time of trouble and uncertainty. Sin abounds and life can get scary. But God steps in, like He did in the time of the exodus. He offers protection, shade, and shelter.

May we find shelter in His presence today and every day until He comes.

*All Scripture quotations are taken from *The Message*, copyright © 1993, 2002, 2018 by Eugene H. Peterson. Used by permission of NavPress. All rights reserved. Represented by Tyndale House Publishers.

MAKING IT REAL

If you've never done it before, take some time to make some unleavened bread. It's easy to do and if you have children, it's a wonderful way to tell the story of the exodus as well as have some fun as a family. Find the simple recipe on our website: **startingwithjesus.com/lesson-21-free-at-last/**

Only God

can provide
a way to bring calm
to your storm.

WEEK TWENTY-TWO

God's Promises at Marah

READ **EXODUS 15:22-27**

Exodus 15:23, 24 *Now when they came to Marah, they could not drink the waters of Marah, for they were bitter. Therefore the name of it was called Marah. And the people complained against Moses, saying, "What shall we drink?"*

RENEW YOUR MIND

My husband and I decided we needed a change of scenery that wouldn't involve a lot of time or money. We located a new and interesting place to explore in a nearby state. Everything we read looked like this town would provide just the right mix—a little history, some shops, and a few quaint restaurants. Expectations were high as we set out.

> **Their problem was that their expectations were not fixed on the Cloud ahead of them. Expectations without God will always end short.**

We arrived or so said the GPS, but nothing was as we anticipated. We checked the signs, and while they said the name of the town, it was nothing like we expected. No little shops; a not-so-appealing restaurant; and one gas station.

This was the Israelite experience. They talked as they walked about what they would see, the food they would eat, and best of all, freedom. Expectations were high. Three days later, not so much. They were tired. Their throats were parched. The scenery was all sand and no beach. This was not what was advertised.

It wasn't, however, their expectations that caused their discontent, although if set too high they can lead to serious disappointment. Their problem was that their expectations were not fixed on the Cloud ahead of them. Expectations without God will always end short. God knew the need for water. He knew the body and the spirit needed to be quenched. He led them to water, but in a way that required that they recognize how they got there and Who provided it. In setting their minds simply on their thirst, they lost the greater lesson.

So how is it with you today? Feeling parched? Thirst can push us in directions that God never intended if we don't connect our need of Him with our needs for today. Put all your expectations in God whether for yourself, your children, your goals, your desires, your needs. Discover the water He is providing—not water that is bitter, but the water that is sweet and satisfying because He has given it just for you. Drink full. Drink long. Be renewed.

FURTHER READING

Patriarchs and Prophets, pages 291-292

The Story of Redemption, page 126

The Bible Story, vol. 2, pages 139-140

Renew YOUR SPIRIT

make new • restore • replenish • reestablish • revive

DIGGING DEEPER

The New Testament is full of stories about those who struggled with expectations particularly when it came to Jesus. Remember John the Baptist? He was a firebrand for God, but when he found himself languishing in a dark, damp prison, he sent his disciples to Jesus to ask, "Are you the one who is to come, or should we expect someone else?" (Matt. 11:3, NIV).

> When things aren't going well, it's not because God isn't working.

We are not unlike John. Even as strong believers, when things are not going as expected, we wonder why God has not acted in the way He has promised. We want Him to do what we want, when we want it, and meet our expectations because we have lived as He has asked. From our perspective, it seems fair. I do what You asked. Then You must do what I expect. And now who's in charge of our future? It isn't God.

Notice Jesus' response to John: "Blessed is anyone who does not stumble on account of me" (verse 6). When things aren't going well, it's not because God isn't working. It's that our ability to see isn't clear. Pray for understanding. Ask God to help you follow His plan even if it isn't where you expect to be led.

MAKING IT REAL

For worship, read these verses on expectation. **Are hope and expectation related? How?**

Psalm 5:3
Psalm 62:5
Proverbs 11:7
Jeremiah 29:11
Luke 3:15-16
Luke 12:40
Romans 8:19
Romans 8:25
2 Corinthians 8:5
Philippians 1:20

Follow His plan

even if it isn't where you expect to be led.

WEEK TWENTY-THREE

Food From Heaven

READ **EXODUS 16**

Exodus 16:23 *Then he said to them, "This is what the Lord has said: 'Tomorrow is a Sabbath rest, a holy Sabbath to the Lord. Bake what you will bake today, and boil what you will boil; and lay up for yourselves all that remains, to be kept until morning.'"*

RENEW YOUR MIND

My daughter is a music teacher. There are times when she gets so excited about how her ensembles are doing she will bubble over with "music talk." Recently we had one of those moments as she shared a piece of music that, for her high school students, was challenging. It wasn't difficult because of the notes or the tempo, but because of the rhythm. The music told a story

> The steady beat of God's metronome: 1-2-3-4-5-6, rest. 1-2-3-4-5-6, rest. 1-2-3-4-5-6-rest.

and as the story reached a moment of chaos, the time signature changed from 4/4 to 6/8 to 2/4 to 9/8 to 7/8 multiple times (musicians will appreciate this detail). In order for the "chaos" to be what the composer intended; the students must watch the director.

Band students don't arrive at class knowing how to do this. It takes time and practice. At first it is all about the steady beat—playing simple songs to simple rhythms as the director taps the beat on the music stand. One, two, three, four. One, two, three, four. One, two, three, four.

The Israelites had been traveling for six weeks. Still a diverse group with strong ties to Egypt and memories that weren't always reliable, they grumbled. This time not for water, but for food. But note God's response. He does not scold. He does not get angry. Instead, He gives them a "steady beat."

New in their relationship together, God could not expect advanced understanding. They must first learn the rhythm of His song. This is what manna did for them. Each day they collected an amount of food that was enough for that day. On the seventh day they rested. The steady beat of God's metronome: 1-2-3-4-5-6, rest. 1-2-3-4-5-6, rest. 1-2-3-4-5-6-rest. This song, their song, would be practiced for the next 40 years.

We, too, must learn the rhythm of God's song. It continues to echo down the millennia to our day. Our manna is found in the Word, our daily bread in Jesus, the Bread of Life. But, like the Israelites, we must continue to practice: 1-2-3-4-5-6, rest. The rest is an important part of the rhythm, as is following the Director.

Each day gather what is needed to sustain your soul. Don't forget the Sabbath, your day to rest. Most importantly, keep an eye on the Director for when the chaos comes, you will be ready to play.

FURTHER READING

Patriarchs and Prophets, pages 292-297

The Story of Redemption, pages 126-131

The Bible Story, vol. 2, pages 140-145

Renew YOUR SPIRIT

make new • restore • replenish • reestablish • revive

DIGGING DEEPER

Many think that the Sabbath wasn't instituted by God until He gave the 10 commandments to Moses on Mt. Sinai. This isn't true, as is evident in this week's lesson. Six weeks after the Israelites left Egypt God instituted the Sabbath, a constant reminder of His care as well as His sovereignty as Creator. Note what we learn about the Sabbath in these verses from Exodus 16:

> Six weeks after the Israelites left Egypt God instituted the Sabbath.

- The Sabbath is the seventh day (verses 22, 23, 26, 29).
- There should be preparation for the Sabbath (verses 22, 23).
- The Sabbath is a holy day (verse 23).
- The Sabbath is a day of rest (verses 23, 29, 30).
- This Sabbath is a command from God (verses 23, 28).
- The Sabbath is to be kept to honor (remember) the Lord. (verses 23, 25).
- Everyone is to stay where he is on the Sabbath (verse 29).
- The Lord gave the Sabbath to man (verse 29).

MAKING IT REAL

Each week should have a rhythm such that when the Sabbath arrives, things are noticeably different. Different atmosphere, different routine, different food, different activities. If you have not yet created a special way to celebrate and honor the Sabbath, think of ways this week to do just that.

For those with younger children, what could you do each day that would prepare for the Sabbath to help them understand the rhythm and the rest? Remember, adults need rhythm too. No kids? Think of ways you can prepare for the Sabbath each day. Check out suggestions at **startingwithjesus.com/lesson-23-food-from-heaven/**

We must find
the rhythm of
God's song.

WEEK TWENTY-FOUR

Water From a Rock

READ **EXODUS 17, 18**

Exodus 17:6 *"Behold, I will stand before you there on the rock in Horeb; and you shall strike the rock, and water will come out of it, that the people may drink."*

RENEW YOUR MIND

The last three weeks the lessons and thus our devotionals have been remarkably similar. We have studied three stories about the Israelites that happened in about the same amount of time as our study—one incident right after the other. Three weeks ago, we learned they were complaining. Last week, they were grumbling. This week, quarreling.

Three weeks. Three stories. Similar challenges, but each differs in the intensity of response. There is, however, one constant.

Three weeks ago, their complaints were about water. Last week, food. This week, water again.

Three weeks ago, we watched Moses throw up his hands in distress. Last week he was calmer, but essentially told them (in the original Hebrew) "Shut-up!" This week, he questioned God as to why he was ever put in such a situation.

Three weeks. Three stories. Similar challenges, but each differs in the intensity of response.

There is, however, one constant. God. He does not change His response to the Israelites or Moses in spite of what they do or how they ask. Constant. Steady. Longsuffering.

We've all experienced little people (or big ones) who because they are bored, tired, or sick, even though we love them, become annoying. Annoying leads to irritation. Irritation leads to reactions that probably aren't much different than how Moses felt. In that we can relate. But how amazing is it that we serve a God who responds in spite of it all continually with patience and grace?

In the story of the Israelites, we learn more of God as well as how He works on our behalf. The same shepherd's staff at the burning bush dedicated to His service brought deliverance from Egypt. The same staff opened the Red Sea. The same staff provided refreshment from a rock. He provides today what He did then. While we may not see the staff or sense the Cloud, He still quenches our thirst, sates our hunger, offers us rest, and hears our cries. He, the divine Shepherd, leads us in the "paths of righteousness" each day. And in His constancy, we are renewed.

FURTHER READING

Patriarchs and Prophets, pages 297-301

The Story of Redemption, pages 131-136

The Bible Story, vol. 2, pages 146-150

Renew YOUR SPIRIT

make new • restore • replenish • reestablish • revive

DIGGING DEEPER

A great spiritual truth is found within the story of water from the rock. Paul references it in 1 Corinthians 10:1-4:

> *Jesus is the Rock that we can depend on for our every need.*

"Moreover, brethren, I do not want you to be unaware that all our fathers were under the cloud, all passed through the sea, all were baptized into Moses in the cloud and in the sea, all ate the same spiritual food, and all drank the same spiritual drink. For they drank of that spiritual Rock that followed them, and that Rock was Christ."

The rock that was struck by Moses where water flowed freely to quench their thirst represented Jesus. Jesus is the Rock that we can depend on for our every need. Only water that flows from Him will satisfy our thirst for truth.

Interestingly, Paul references the "Rock that followed them . . .", which we understand as Jesus who was ever-present. Jewish tradition, however, believed that a rock literally did follow the Israelites throughout their 40-year journey through the desert providing them with the water needed. Whether a literal rock followed them or not we do not know, but Ellen White shares, "Wherever in their journeyings they wanted water, there from the clefts of the rock it gushed beside their encampment" (*Patriarchs and Prophets*, p. 411). Each time they needed water they need only look to the Source of refreshment.

MAKING IT REAL

For family worship, read some scriptures that talk about the water of life for our soul. Psalm 42:1, 2; Psalm 63: Isaiah 12:3; John 7:37, 38

Then sing "A Shelter in a Time of Storm" (#528, *The Seventh-day Adventist Hymnal*. If you do not have a hymnal, visit **sdahymnal.org**.) If you don't know the hymn, take time to learn it or read the words out loud.

He is today
what He was then.

WEEK TWENTY-FIVE

God Speaks His Law

READ **EXODUS 19; 20:1-20**

Exodus 19:18 Now Mount Sinai was completely in smoke, because the Lord descended upon it in fire. Its smoke ascended like the smoke of a furnace, and the whole mountain quaked greatly.

RENEW YOUR MIND

The cancer diagnosis came unexpectedly. My husband was a young man and we had two young children. It was the beginning of apprehension, medical appointments, and surgeries. Early on he decided to be anointed. It seemed the right thing to do—take the problem directly to God not later when hope was lost, but in the beginning where confusion and anxiety begged for His presence. We will never forget our pastor's response. Not his lack of acceptance, but the directions. My husband was to select those he wished to surround him during the anointing. For three days prior, all involved were to seek God fervently in prayer and confession, to prepare to meet a Holy God. One individual dropped out because he felt he could not meet the requirements. Exodus 19 became real and applicable. One does not simply walk into the presence of God.

* * *

My oldest daughter was engaged! Immediately the wedding planning began. The usual decisions of date, time, invitations, colors, and venues occupied our time. How she would look was the other. She selected the right dress, arranged for her hair and makeup, and planned for her groom's first glimpse on this important day. For her, it also involved music. She listened to all kinds of music for her bridal processional, until deciding on "Te Deum Prelude" by Marc-Antoine Charpentier.

Everything was planned and orchestrated. As the music began on the pipe organ, the congregation turned expectantly toward the closed doors at the back of the sanctuary. After 20 seconds of anticipation, the organ hit a crescendo as the double doors swung open revealing the bride. She proceeded triumphantly down the aisle toward her groom. At the end of the aisle, there was silence. The next moment would begin the covenant ceremony.

* * *

Exodus 19 and 20 are about God. Often, we are encouraged to think of God as our Best Friend or our Daddy. While He is absolutely one who cares and loves us more than any earthly individual, we must never forget who He is. To stand in the presence of God without being prepared is to forget His ultimate sovereignty. He is the Creator of the world absolutely focused on every minute detail of our lives, sending thousands of angels if necessary to watch and protect us. But He is holy. He reminds the Israelites of this as they prepare to meet Him at the base of Mt. Sinai.

Chapter 20 sets up the divine encounter—the moment before God will speak His covenant in the form of the 10 commandments. A black cloud descends the mountain veiling Jesus with an entourage of angels attending Him. There is thunder, lightning, and the sounds of trumpets followed by silence.

God has arrived.

> She proceeded triumphantly down the aisle toward her groom. At the end of the aisle, there was silence.

FURTHER READING

Patriarchs and Prophets, pages 301-305

The Story of Redemption, pages 137-141

The Bible Story, vol. 2, pages 153-157

Renew YOUR SPIRIT

make new • restore • replenish • reestablish • revive

DIGGING DEEPER

In Exodus 19, we find one example of a theophany. Prior to the coming of Jesus in the New Testament, the Old Testament had theophanies—the appearance of God. In Exodus 19, He appeared in the form of a dark cloud with thunder and lightning. Here are some others:

> The Old Testament had theophanies—the appearance of God.

- Genesis 18: God appeared to Abraham in the form of a man, walking with two others.
- Genesis 32: God appeared to Jacob, again in the form of a man, wrestling with him until daybreak.
- Exodus 3: God appeared in the form of a burning bush.
- Exodus 13: God appeared in the form of a cloudy pillar by day and a pillar of fire by night.
- Job 38: God appeared in a whirlwind and challenged Job by a series of questions.

Prophets such as Isaiah and Ezekiel saw visions of God in His heavenly temple. David may also have had such an experience. Read his account in Psalm 18:6-19.

MAKING IT REAL

God's appearances are not limited to the Bible. Many share stories where God has demonstrated His power on their behalf. A story from Pastor Geoffrey Mbwana, who served as one of the general vice-presidents at the General Conference, is a great one for family worship. Read it here: **adventist.news/news/the-protection-of-god**

We must *never forget* who He is.

H O L Y

WEEK TWENTY-SIX

How We Love God

READ EXODUS 20:1-7

Exodus 20:1, 2 And God spoke all these words, saying: "I am the Lord your God, who brought you out of the land of Egypt, out of the house of bondage."

RENEW YOUR MIND

In 2009, author and speaker Simon Sinek, gave a TED talk entitled, "How Great Leaders Inspire Action." Sinek's intent was to inspire a new way of thinking for corporate America, but after listening, it instead changed the way I read the Bible.

In his presentation, he spoke of the way leaders tend to process. Drawing three circles in the shape of a target, Sinek wrote three familiar terms. In the outer circle, he wrote "What." The middle circle, "How." And the innermost circle, "Why." His conclusion was that the most successful leaders think differently than most—from the inside out. They start with the "why," then state the "how," followed by the "what." To express why something is reveals its overall purpose. It gives intentionality. According to Sinek, only when "why" is understood, does success follow.

So, what does corporate inspiration have to do with the 10 Commandments? Because God uses the exact process Sinek has suggested. Jesus did as well. It explains why the disciples were always confused until after the resurrection and ascension. They continued to ask "what" and "how" questions of Jesus, but His answers were generally always "why." Jesus was completely focused on His mission—the end game—while His disciples were caught in the how. Other Bible stories are similar. Re-read the story of Balaam. Three curses become three blessings, however, at the end, God uses Balaam to give one additional prophecy—the "why."

When one memorizes the 10 commandments, we start with the first one. That would make sense, except that we miss the most important part—the prologue. God comes down the mountain to speak to His people, to establish the principles of His covenant. But before beginning He states the "why": "I am the Lord your God, who brought you out of the land of Egypt, out of the house of bondage" (v. 2).

This declaration is critical because it encapsulates all that is God and why the covenant matters. This one verse completely sums up what has happened in the previous 19 chapters. He is the Deliverer, the Redeemer, the One who rescues. This was the message to the Israelites. It is the same for us today.

Now the commandments of the covenant make sense. We agree with them and with Him because of what He does for us. There are no other gods because no other god can do what He did. We will not make anything or put anything in place of Him because when we do we limit the what and how of what He can do for us. We will reverence His name, because He is holy and just and mighty and powerful. It's the why that makes the difference.

The why helps us understand who we worship. It's the why that renews us each day.

> Only when "why" is understood, does success follow.

FURTHER READING

Patriarchs and Prophets, pages 305-307

The Story of Redemption, page 141

Renew YOUR SPIRIT

make new • restore • replenish • reestablish • revive

DIGGING DEEPER

Jon Dybdahl in his book, *Exodus,* reveals something interesting about the organizational structure of Exodus. Exodus contains several law codes, regulations, or commands, of which the 10 commandments is only one. Each time a law code is revealed it is bracketed by a story.

> "The laws cannot be understood properly without the story."

He writes: "There are four such blocks of law: the Ten Commandments (20:1-17), the covenant code (20:22-23:33), the priesthood code (25:1-31:1-18), and the tabernacle code (35:1-40:33). Each block is preceded and followed by story. The laws cannot be understood properly without the story and vice versa. The very structure of the book makes law and story an integrated whole."

He goes on to explain the significance of this structure:

- God becomes the primary force in both story and commands.
- The law is more fully seen as a gift from God when tied to a story that illustrates His mercy and deliverance.
- The motivation to keep the law is found within the story.
- Law and story join together to help us see the combination of divine action with human response as it pertains to life.

*Dybdahl, John, *Exodus*, part of The Abundant Life Bible Amplifier series, Pacific Press Publishing Association, 1994.

MAKING IT REAL

Consider the first three commandments and answer these questions about them:
1. How is God the one true God in your life?
2. How do you place God first in all you do?
3. How do you keep God's name holy?

He is the Deliverer,
the Redeemer,
*the One
who rescues.*

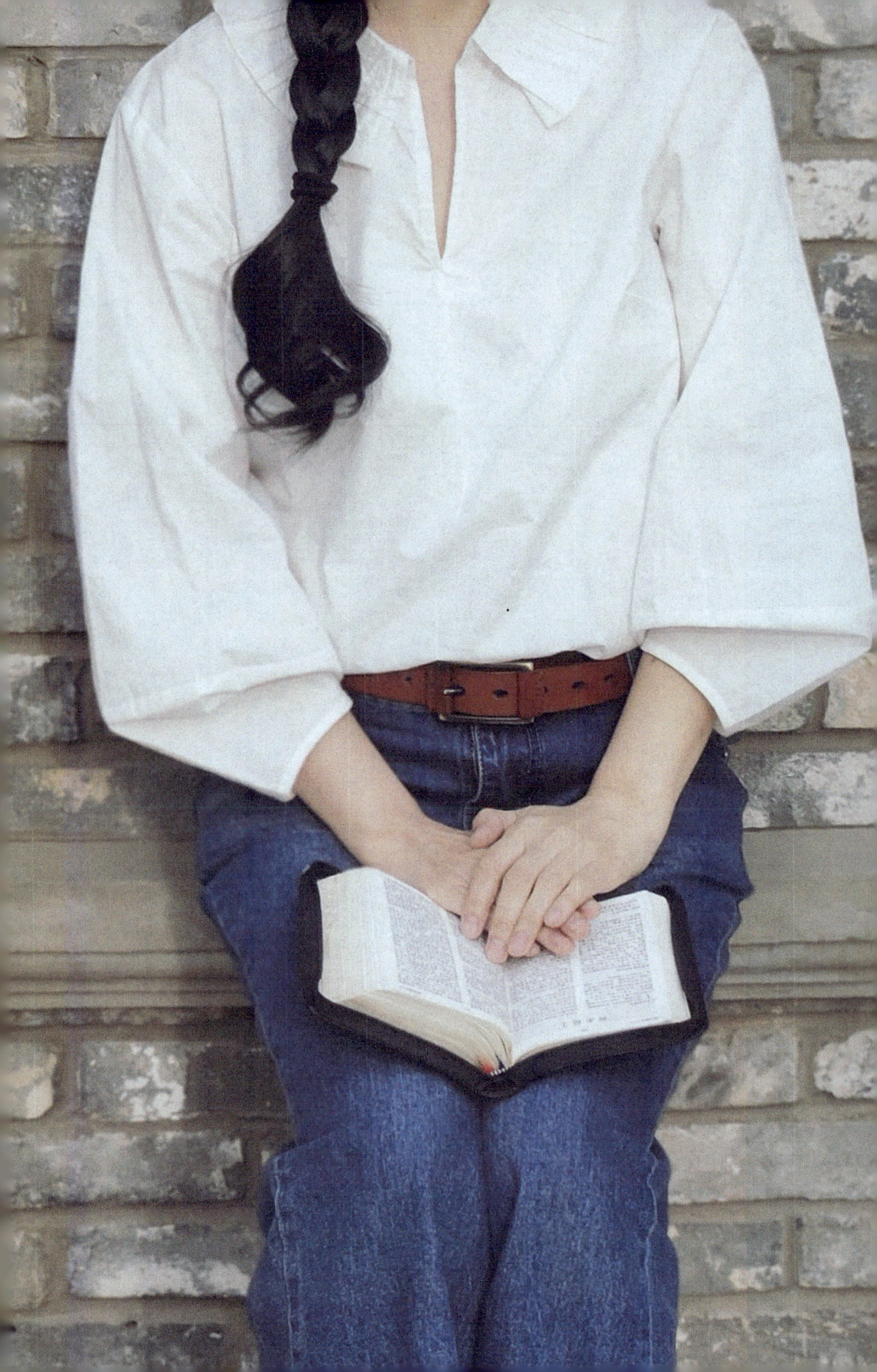

PART THREE

Following His Plan

WEEK TWENTY-SEVEN

Remember God's Special Day

READ **EXODUS 20:8-11**

Exodus 20:8 "*Remember the Sabbath day, to keep it holy.*"

RENEW YOUR MIND

I don't live far from Washington, D.C., the capital of the United States. If you were to drive into the city it wouldn't be long before you saw the first memorial. It seems that on every corner is a monument to something or someone that has some significance in this nation's history. The Lincoln Memorial, the Jefferson Memorial, the Washington Monument, the World War II Memorial, the Vietnam Veterans Memorial, and on it goes. They are there to cause us to remember.

The fourth commandment is something like those memorials. Each time the seventh day of the week, Sabbath (Saturday), comes we are to be reminded. Not only are we to remember, but we are also to remind our children. Just as you might answer their questions about why a monument is there, you also share with them why we make the Sabbath a special day.

We keep the Sabbath to remember God as the Creator. Only He could speak the world into existence. Only by Him does it continue to spin, cause the sun to shine and the air to sustain. We keep the Sabbath by resting. Not literally spending the day in bed, but we remember that once God finished His Creation, He rested. Therefore, we rest in the knowledge of His abundant love and grace for us.

Recently I had a to-do list that seemed to have no end. As the day was coming to a close, I knew the next item had an immediate deadline and rest would not come until it was completed. Just then my phone chirped. It was my daughter texting she had actually done the next item for me! Filled with surprise and relief, I sent her profuse thanks. Because she did the work, I was free to rest.

And that's when it occurred to me that I've missed another important lesson from the Sabbath. When I rest on the Sabbath, God does not. He continues to work on our behalf. I can be relieved of work, worries, or tragic headlines because God is in control. Because He is, we are safe, loved, and protected. We rest in arms that hold us securely forever and ever. Being reminded of this once a week is good for my soul.

The Washington Monument has stood for almost 175 years. Rock solid, it appears immovable. And yet, in 2011, an earthquake damaged the monument, a reminder that these memorials are only one terrible event from bringing them crashing down. What man has built, while meaningful, is fallible. Not so the Sabbath. The Sabbath, like God, is a constant. It remains a true memorial to the beginning of time. Let us remember, rest, remain, and be renewed.

He continues to work on our behalf.

FURTHER READING

Patriarchs and Prophets, pages 307-308

The Story of Redemption, pages 141-142

Renew YOUR SPIRIT

make new • restore • replenish • reestablish • revive

DIGGING DEEPER

If you are like me, when the Sabbath rolls around you experience joy, relief, and excitement. But I must confess that, for me, it isn't always for the right reasons. It often stems from the absence of work as well as the absence of chores. While I might sink into a chair knowing that there are six piles of laundry calling my name, I can ignore them in comfort and bliss.

> The Sabbath was never intended as a day of idleness and inactivity.

While rest and absence of labor is certainly part of the Sabbath commandment, the *Seventh-day Adventist Bible Commentary* expands the meaning of rest.

> "We should 'remember' also that mere rest from physical labor does not constitute Sabbath observance. The Sabbath was never intended as a day of idleness and inactivity. Sabbathkeeping is not so much a matter of refraining from certain forms of activity as it is of entering purposefully into others. We cease from the weekly round of toil only as a means to the end of devoting the day to other pursuits. The spirit of true Sabbathkeeping will lead one to improve its sacred hours by seeking to understand more perfectly the character and will of God, to appreciate more fully His love and mercy, and to cooperate more effectively with Him in ministering to the spiritual needs of his fellow men" (vol. 1, p. 604).

MAKING IT REAL

After reading the above quote, **what kind of activity could you plan** for this coming Sabbath that either helps you understand God better, helps you appreciate His love and mercy, or helps to minister to the spiritual needs of others?

We rest

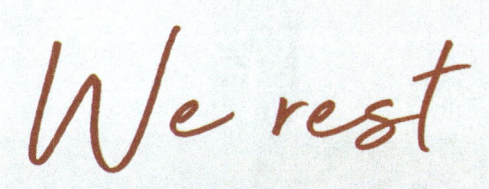

in arms that hold us securely forever and ever.

WEEK TWENTY-EIGHT

How We Love Others

READ **EXODUS 20:12-17**

Exodus 20:13-16 *"You shall not murder. You shall not commit adultery. You shall not steal. You shall not bear false witness against your neighbor."*

RENEW YOUR MIND

The past two lessons have covered the commandments that pertain to God. We now move to the second stone tablet with six additional commandments that relate to how we treat others. In short, we should treat our parents well, respect life, honor marriage, not take what doesn't belong to us, tell the truth, and not yearn for something that is not ours. Keeping these will lead toward a happy, contented life. While all six are important, I would like to focus on one in a way you may not have considered.

Two quick stories about my youngest daughter. First, she is tall and always has been. I knew that if I didn't help her early on to see the value of height, she might become self-conscious rounding her shoulders and slouching in an attempt to make herself "small" like her friends. At about three years of age, I began to tell her, "You will be a beautifully tall young woman one day." She would smile having no idea what I was talking about but taking it as the compliment it was. As often as I could I would repeat this to her, until the day I dreaded arrived—sixth grade. She had the growth spurt I anticipated and she now towered over her shorter friends. But she carried herself tall and proud. Straight back, shoulders even, like a model. Why? Because she saw herself, in spite of the middle school awkwardness, what had been prophesied—she was tall and beautiful.

Same daughter, different story. She had hit a challenging phase in her development. I don't remember the age, but I do remember the behavior—argumentative, uncooperative, and, if honest, not particularly likeable. That always comes as a surprise when parents face the fact that truth be told, they aren't especially enamored with what their child has become even when they know it will pass. I was reaching a place of exasperation when I decided to do something. Every day at some opportune moment I would say to her, "You know what I like about you . . .?" Her face would brighten, and she would say, "What?" And then I would respond (if you try this, make sure you have an answer!) After several days of this, I recognized something. I no longer saw my daughter's behavior as a trial because I was looking for something to say. I was looking for the good and didn't see the "bad."

The sixth commandment says, "You shall not murder" or in other translations, "kill." We typically think of this as taking a life. But Jesus expanded it to include anger and dislike (Matt. 5:21, 22). John later added "hatred" (1 John 3:14, 15). We must be careful of our words. Words can injure another in ways that are almost worse than taking their life. When you "kill" the spirit of another, you wound them in ways that are far-reaching and many never recover.

Watch your words. Find ways to use them to build up your children (no matter how old they are), your spouse, and those around you. Kind words can water the soul, nurture the spirit, and when used effectively bring renewal not only to ourselves, but to others. ⑬

> She saw herself, in spite of the middle school awkwardness, what had been prophesied— she was tall and beautiful.

FURTHER READING

Patriarchs and Prophets, pages 308-309

Renew YOUR SPIRIT

make new • restore • replenish • reestablish • revive

DIGGING DEEPER

The tenth commandment is an interesting one. Where all the others are actions to be done or to be avoided, the last commandment actually speaks to motive or thought. To covet

The Sabbath was never intended as a day of idleness and inactivity.

someone else's possessions is to think about what they have that is better than yours and then take the step of wanting it for yourself. It's the last commandment that will lead you to break number 8, which can lead to breaking number 9. Of course, if you break 8, 9, and 10, you will have dishonored God in the process breaking the first three. And so it goes.

Remember the words of God to Samuel that man looks on the outward appearance, but the Lord looks on the heart. We must be careful of becoming discontented. Where our hearts are can lead us in the wrong direction.

MAKING IT REAL

The very first commandment after those that honor God is one that honors our parents. Parents represent God to their children. Good parenting reflects well on Him; poor parenting can have disastrous effects. Not all are blessed with parents that have taught them well and treated them kindly.

If you were blessed to have such parents and they are still alive, call them now and spend some time with them. Or buy a card or write a letter of appreciation and thanks.

If you struggled with your parents, and perhaps there is distance between you, is there something you can do to reach out to them? Is there a way you can represent the kindness of Jesus to them in spite of the broken relationship?

If your parents have passed, be thankful for the memories that you have. Maybe spend some time looking at an old photo album. Tell some stories to your children. Demonstrate to them how to "honor parents."

Kind words
can water the soul.

WEEK TWENTY-NINE

Broken Promises

READ **EXODUS 24, 32, 34**

Exodus 32:24 "*And I said to them, 'Whoever has any gold, let them break it off.' So they gave it to me, and I cast it into the fire, and this calf came out.*"

RENEW YOUR MIND

There's a recipe website I sometimes visit. When I find one with potential, I always read the comments first to find tips that might make the dish tastier. What never ceases to amaze me are those reviewers who write something like this:

"I didn't have [x] so I substituted [y]. My family doesn't like [a] so I used [b]. Instead of boiling, we fried it. It was delicious! Definitely making this recipe again!"

I have to laugh because they didn't actually make the recipe but created their own and called it by the same name!

The golden calf experience is a low point in Israel's history. It had only been weeks since Israel made a covenant with God to keep His commandments. How did it devolve into such a mess?

I could write about the art of waiting, clearly something they didn't do well. I could write about the choice of friends—according to Ellen White it all started with the mixed multitude from Egypt (*Patriarchs and Prophets*, p. 316). I could even write about the danger of setting up an idol. While all of that would be applicable, it was actually more subtle and dangerous.

The people came to Aaron with a problem. Moses was gone, probably dead, and, they added, there was no God as well. Aaron did something interesting. Instead of stopping things right where they started, he accommodated them. But notice he doesn't come out and agree with them entirely. The people credited the golden calf with leading them out of Egypt (Exodus 32:4). But Aaron did not (v. 5). Aaron didn't take God away, he simply added. Where God instructed Israel on who He was and how He was to be worshiped, Aaron added the calf, the altar, and the festival all to *honor God*.

None of us are worried about setting up a golden anything in our living room. But are we susceptible to voices that suggest how we worship, where we worship, or on what day we worship? Voices that say it doesn't matter what we do as long as God is honored? In this, we are no different than the cook who alters the recipe to their own liking. The goal may be to make the Special K loaf, but after the substitutions and alterations, is it really the original recipe or one of your own creation?

There is always danger when we add to God's plan, whether due to impatience, listening to those not truly converted, or because we fashion our own way to worship. God requires our full attention as well as our commitment. He loves, provides, and has expectations for us. His commandments are not negotiable. They are not a recipe to simply alter because of taste or allergic reactions. Learn of God. Learn of His love. Then like David, we can say, "Oh, taste and see that the Lord is good!" (Psalm 34:7). ⓑ

There is always danger when we add to God's plan.

FURTHER READING

Patriarchs and Prophets, pages 309-342, 363-373

The Story of Redemption, pages 142-150

The Bible Story, vol. 2, pages 157-176

Renew YOUR SPIRIT

make new • restore • replenish • reestablish • revive

DIGGING DEEPER

Something interesting happens in Exodus 32 that you don't want to miss. Moses is absent during the golden calf experience. He finds out about it from God, Himself, who tells him to go down to the camp because the people have rejected God and bowed to a calf. That must have been startling news for Moses to hear, but the next words catch his attention. "Now therefore, let Me alone, that My wrath may burn hot against them and I may consume them. And I will make of you a great nation" (verses 9, 10). Moses doesn't appear shaken by the news, or God's response. Instead, he pleads with God that this is not the best plan.

> **To sacrifice Moses would not redeem the nation because he was a sinner in need of atonement himself.**

God relents and Moses heads down the mountain where the sight of the people and their sin angers him as it did God. He broke the commandments, melted the calf, mandated the drinking of the gold powder, and called for the killing of 3,000 people who stood in rebellion. But Moses was not finished.

Moses had spent 40 days with God learning about the tabernacle. The purpose of the sanctuary was atonement—the offering of a sacrifice to remove sin that stood between the people and God. While the sanctuary was yet in the future, Moses recognized their great sin required atonement. How could this be accomplished? Verses 30-31 tell us. Moses offered himself!

Moses understood God's plan of salvation enough to recognize that in order to reestablish the relationship with God, a sacrifice was needed, not an animal, but a man—one person for the nation. What he failed to grasp was that he was not qualified. To sacrifice Moses would not redeem the nation because he was a sinner in need of atonement himself. Only Jesus, the sinless, spotless Lamb of God, could do this. So here we find in Exodus the heart of the gospel, thousands of years before Jesus came to earth. The plan of salvation was revealed—a glimpse of the sacrifice that would be given for them and for us, not by an ordinary man, but God Himself.

Follow His recipe;
follow His plan.

MAKING IT REAL

Moses was willing to sacrifice himself for his people. That showed a deep level of commitment to the leadership God had called him to do. Think about your level of sacrifice. **What would you be willing to do for Jesus?**

WEEK THIRTY

A Dwelling Place for God

READ   **EXODUS 25-31**

Exodus 29:43 *"And there I will meet with the children of Israel, and the tabernacle shall be sanctified by My glory."*

RENEW YOUR MIND

You're probably aware of the superhero phenomena. The revenue on anything related to superheroes is in the billions of dollars whether it is spent at the movie theater box office or Target. People love these heroes who with their special powers arrive at the last minute to save an individual, a city, or the world.

God was not a superhero that watched from afar, but a God that would live with them in the center of their camp.

The Israelites seem to have some superhero issues of their own. For them, God lived at the top of a mountain—a mountain they were forbidden to enter. And while there were occasional black clouds, thunder, and lightning, He seemed distant. With Moses gone for so long at the top of this mountain, doubt suggested that not only was Moses probably dead, but this God might not show up when you needed Him.

Of course, their memories were short and their eyes dim. The pillar of cloud that gave shade by day, and warmth by night was God. The miracles that He had done to rescue and redeem them were far too many to count. While God's plan was unfolding piece by piece, the ability to keep God in focus and fully present seemed to be challenging and problematic. In their doubt and unbelief, they created another god—one that could not see, hear, act, or redeem, but was right in front of them somehow making it "real."

Unfortunately, for the Israelites, their lack of patience got the better of them. On the mountain, God was telling Moses what would happen next. Moses and the people were to build a tabernacle, a sanctuary for God to dwell. God would "tabernacle" with them, the very word itself meaning "to be in the midst." God was not a superhero that watched from afar, but a God that would live with them in the center of their camp.

I hope you are thinking what I am. What God did symbolically there in the desert, He did for real two thousand years later. Jesus, God's Son, came to earth to live "in the midst" of His people. He came to walk, talk, heal, teach, preach, live, and die among us. His name, "God with us," took the idea of "tabernacle" to a whole new level.

God with us. One cannot help but be renewed.

FURTHER READING

Patriarchs and Prophets, pages 343-358; 363-373

The Story of Redemption, pages 151-157

The Bible Story, vol. 2, pages 177-187

Renew YOUR SPIRIT

make new • restore • replenish • reestablish • revive

DIGGING DEEPER

The wilderness tabernacle occupies 13 chapters in Exodus, almost a third of the entire book. You will find it twice—first in the plans given to Moses by God on the mountain, and then when they actually built it. What separates the two accounts are three important chapters.

> Notice that Moses was on the mountain 40 days and 40 nights, exactly the length of the first time, but this had a very different ending.

Chapter 32 is the golden calf experience. This apostasy was so great that God at first threatened to destroy the entire nation and start over with Moses. Moses sought atonement from God at the end of the chapter and all seemed well, until you begin chapter 33.

In the very first verses, God agreed to His promise. He directed them to leave and go to the Promise Land. He would provide an angel to lead them, but He would not go with them! This declaration seemed to finally penetrate the hearts of the people for they fell into great mourning. They removed their jewelry and showed repentance for their sin.

In addition, a "tent of meeting" was set up, not one that took the place of the tabernacle, but one that allowed God to meet with Moses and the people instead of Moses always having to climb the mountain. But note its placement —outside the camp (33:7). This was an important reminder of their sin. As Moses went to enter the tent, all the people watched to see if their leader would be accepted. An invitation was given to the people, that all who had a repentant heart might approach the tent of meeting.

Chapter 34 then speaks of a time when the covenant was renewed. Moses received a new set of tablets containing the law. He entreated God to lead them again, to pardon their sin, and accept them as His people. Notice that Moses was on the mountain 40 days and 40 nights, exactly the length of the first time, but this had a very different ending. He came down the mountain with the law again, and the covenant with God was renewed. Then and only then could the building of the tabernacle begin.

Experience *"God with us."*

> **MAKING IT REAL**

Maybe you've heard the expression "pray in your closet." It's an expression that speaks of a time alone with God with no distractions—a "tent of meeting" if you will. Do you have a "tent of meeting," a place and a time where you can meet and talk with God without being disturbed? If not, where could it be? Perhaps in the shower or your bed before drifting off to sleep or first thing waking in the morning could be your special time. Maybe it's nursing the baby in the wee hours of a dark morning. Maybe it's mowing the lawn. Where can you go and be undisturbed as you commune with God?

WEEK THIRTY-ONE

God's Beautiful Sanctuary

READ **EXODUS 35; 36; 39:32-40**

Exodus 39:32 *Thus all the work of the tabernacle of the tent of meeting was finished. And the children of Israel did according to all that the Lord had commanded Moses; so they did.*

RENEW YOUR MIND

There are some extremely detailed chapters in the Bible whether they be ancestry, land boundaries, or sacrificial offerings and we wonder why we should care. In fact, if honest, we may admit to skipping right over them.

This could be a temptation in Exodus as we reach the detailed description of the wilderness sanctuary. To do so will mean skipping about a third of the book. And the information is repeated twice! Is it that important? Let's review.

Altar of Sacrifice: The altar was found in the outer court near the entrance. Here the people would bring their sacrifices. The blood of the sacrifice was placed on the horns of the altar found at each corner.

Laver: This bronze basin was made from the mirrors supplied by the Israelite women. It held water for cleansing either before the priests performed a sacrifice or before they entered the sanctuary.

Golden Table: The sanctuary sat in the wilderness with the outer court in the east and the Most Holy place in the west. The table, overlaid with gold, was inside the first compartment to the north. On it were placed 12 loaves of bread in two stacks of six.

Lampstand: The lampstand was found on the south side of the Holy Place across from the table. There were three branches off each side ending with a cup in the shape of an almond flower. There was an additional cup at the top for a total of seven lamps. The lampstand remained lit at all times.

Altar of Incense: This stood directly in front of the curtain that separated the Holy Place from the Most Holy Place. The priests burned incense twice a day. It was at this altar where the priests or Moses met with God.

Ark of the Covenant: This box was overlaid with gold and held the Ten Commandments—the law. It was the only piece of furniture found in the Most Holy place. No one was to enter this part of the sanctuary ever with one exception, on the Day of Atonement.

Still wondering why you should care? It's all about the symbolism and all of it points in one direction.

The Israelites had access to God through the altar. Here they would confess their sins and ask for forgiveness. Jesus' death on the cross (**altar**) is where our sins were placed; it is through His blood we are saved.

We wash our sins away through baptism. It is through baptism we are symbolically cleansed, just as the priests cleansed themselves before God (**laver**).

The bread on the **table** represented the care of God for His people supplying all their needs in a desert wilderness. Jesus is the bread of life. He provides all we need or want.

Just as the **lamp** never went out, God is ever-present and watchful, never sleeping, ever alert to our needs.

The **incense** filled the tabernacle with a lovely perfume representing the prayers of the people and continual intercession before God of the needs of the people. Jesus is our advocate and continual representative to God, the Father. Even now, He intercedes on our behalf in the heavenly sanctuary, bringing our petitions to God.

The **ark** represented the relationship—the covenant—of God with His people. He came to dwell with them, to be "in the midst of them." Later Jesus came to be in our midst, not behind a curtain, but Immanuel—"God with us."

Did you hear the message? It's all about Jesus. And that, my friends, is too important to miss. Ⓑ

> It's all about the symbolism and all the symbols point in one direction.

FURTHER READING

Patriarchs and Prophets, pages 343-358; 363-373

The Story of Redemption, pages 151-157

The Bible Story, vol. 2, pages 177-187

Renew YOUR SPIRIT

make new • restore • replenish • reestablish • revive

DIGGING DEEPER

Did you know that when Moses ascended Mount Sinai to receive the law the second time, Jesus was revealed to him?

The people were unable to look upon his face.

"In the mount, when the law was given to Moses, the Coming One was shown to him also. He saw Christ's work, and His mission to earth, when the Son of God should take upon Himself humanity and become a teacher and a guide to the world, and at last give Himself a ransom for their sins. When the perfect Offering should be made for the sins of men, the sacrificial offerings typifying the work of the Messiah were to cease. With the advent of Christ, the veil of uncertainty was to be lifted, and a flood of light shed upon the darkened understanding of His people.

"As Moses saw the day of Christ, and the new and living way of salvation that was to be opened through His blood, he was captivated and entranced. The praise of God was in his heart, and the divine glory that attended the giving of the law was so strikingly revealed in his countenance when he came down from the mount to walk with Israel, that the brightness was painful. Because of their transgressions, the people were unable to look upon his face, and he wore a veil that he might not terrify them. . . .

"Had the Israelites discerned the gospel light that was opened to Moses, had they been able by faith to look steadfastly to the end of that which was abolished, they could have endured the light which was reflected from the countenance of Moses." (*The Signs of the Times*, August 25, 1887).

MAKING IT REAL

Moses face shone coming down the mountain because he grasped the plan of salvation. Already in a close relationship with God, when he saw the tremendous gift of Jesus to the human race in order to save them, he could not help but love Him even more.

Think today about how much God loves you, how much He sacrificed for you. Find ways to praise Him today in song, writing, or deeds.

It's all about

Jesus.

WEEK THIRTY-TWO

Nadab and Abihu

READ **EXODUS 28; 29; 39:1-31; LEVITICUS 8-10**

Leviticus 10:1 *Then Nadab and Abihu, the sons of Aaron, each took his censer and put fire in it, put incense on it, and offered profane fire before the Lord, which He had not commanded them.*

RENEW YOUR MIND

The five colored rings and Olympic flame are familiar sights at the Olympic Games. Tradition requires the cauldron at the games to be lit only by a flame that has been kindled by the sun in Athens, Greece, and then transported by relay to wherever the games are held. This same cauldron is to be seen at all times during the games, thus it is positioned where it is clearly visible.

The idea of a continuous Olympic flame is a meaningful tradition to those who support the Games. Great emphasis and protection is given to the torch that bears the fire to ensure that it never goes out. The same with the cauldron. Once lit, it is to remain that way throughout the games.

The cauldron was lit as custom required at the Montreal Games in 1976. Days later, a sudden storm snuffed out the flame. A nearby plumber, eager to help, pulled out his cigarette lighter instantly solving the problem. That is, until the organizers found out. Horrified, they quickly extinguished the flame and relit the cauldron with a standby torch.

We may smile at this modern story of strange fire. What difference does it make whether the fire comes from Greece or a lighter? Fire is fire. But to Olympic purists, maintaining almost a century of tradition means a great deal. This week's story is also about strange fire, not from a lighter, but another source. The source of the fire also meant a great deal to God enough that He not only extinguished the flame, but also the lives of those who held the fire.

God gave explicit instructions for how Israel was to worship. Nadab and Abihu had been set apart along with their father and brothers to serve as priests, anointed as sacred workers of the sanctuary. They also served as representatives of the people to God, so what they did mattered. Each detail was important; each duty an example. Each instruction symbolic of the greater gift of salvation from God for man.

Yet Nadab and Abihu blurred the sacred with the common. Instead of following God's instruction, they did it their own way at their own time with their own fire, not with the fire from the altar that was lit by God Himself. This was no small thing in the eyes of God. It was direct disobedience and a misrepresentation of all that is sacred.

This is not a happy story by any accounts, but it teaches us a lesson that may run contrary to what people might say. It is not unusual for us to convince ourselves that details aren't that important, that what we do, what we wear, where we go, what we read, think, or say, are not as important as long as God is first in our life. We convince ourselves there is no disconnect in loving God, when we do what works best for us, because He will (or does) understand. This story reminds us that small things matter in heaven's eyes. There is the sacred: who, why, what, and where we worship. There is the common: the things we do whether work, school, or play. God grants both, but we must not confuse Him with the every day. Be careful about the small things. Look up and be renewed.

> **Nadab and Abihu served as representatives of the people to God, so what they did mattered. Each detail was important; each duty an example.**

FURTHER READING

Patriarchs and Prophets, pages 359-373

The Bible Story, vol. 3, pages 9-12

Renew YOUR SPIRIT

make new • restore • replenish • reestablish • revive

DIGGING DEEPER

Nadab and Abihu, as the sons of Aaron, were afforded opportunities that others were not. They had heard the voice of God; they had been up on the top of Mt. Sinai; and they had the supreme honor and privilege of "eating and drinking" with God as well as seeing His glory (Exodus 24:9-11). Prior to the event that culminated in their death, they had spent time learning of the role of the priest as well as the mediatorial work on behalf of the people. Immediately prior to this they had been ordained and blood from the altar had been sprinkled on them in a sacred service.

> How could they have misunderstood what they were to do? More importantly, how could they simply discard the holiness and reverence of God?

This makes one wonder at their actions. How could they have misunderstood what they were to do? More importantly, how could they simply discard the holiness and reverence of God? The answer lies in the line that is drawn between the sacred and the common. While they had gone through all these experiences, had been taught all that was needed to understand and recognize their sacred responsibilities, they remained "common." There was no conversion of the heart, no real recognition and acceptance of a Holy God.

While the Bible does not reveal that Nadab and Abihu were under the influence of alcohol when they chose to put "strange fire" in their censors, it is sometimes connected by Bible commentators because of the admonition given in verse 9. It would suggest that this is not random instruction, but directly related to the preceding event. Ellen White states that, indeed, this was the case (*Patriarchs and Prophets*, p. 361). In becoming intoxicated, their reason was affected and their ability to make wise and solemn choices was affected. In a deteriorated state, their minds could no longer see the difference between what was sacred and belonged to God, and what was common.

Small things matter in heaven's eyes.

MAKING IT REAL

Probably the hardest part of this story is that Aaron was not allowed to grieve the loss of his sons. This was because of their great sin against God. Aaron's grief was doubly compounded because he recognized that his sons were out of control because he had not done his duties as a father in teaching them self-discipline, respect for authority, and reverence for God.

This is a challenging story for a parent because it causes us to do some soul-searching. This week's lesson requires us to take some time to think, pray, and talk about how we are leading our children to Jesus.

- **How can we teach ourselves** to distinguish between the sacred and the common?
- **How can we share what we've learned** with our children?
- **How can we demonstrate the difference** between sacred time or space to common time or space?
- **What kind of things can we do to teach** our children that the sanctuary is a place for worship?
- **Ask am I consistent in my discipline of my children?** Am I teaching them how to be self-disciplined?
- **Offer different scenarios to your child** (appropriate for their age) that teach them how to make good choices.

WEEK THIRTY-THREE

Two Brave Spies

READ **NUMBERS 10-14**

Numbers 13:33 *"There we saw the giants (the descendants of Anak came from the giants); and were like grasshoppers in our own sight, and so we were in their sight."*

RENEW YOUR MIND

It wasn't that the idea to explore the promised land was a bad plan; it was simply incomplete. The people told Moses they wanted to scout out the land (Deut. 1:22), when what they really should have said is "Let us go scout out the land *God has promised*." The addition of those three words changes everything. Had they said this they would have returned reporting on the promise. Instead, they focused on the problem. Their report had everything to do with perspective. That is, except for two.

Caleb and Joshua clearly went with God as part of their mission. Thus, their report included only the possible, not the impossible. They had no additional insight than the others. How giants would disappear, walls fall down, or nations surrender was unknown to them, but what they did know was they had walked out with the spoils of Egypt without a fight. They walked through the Rea Sea on dry ground. They gathered manna in the morning and drank water from a rock. A God that can do those things, can certainly do what seems impossible.

Before we are too quick to criticize the 10 with limited vision, we need to take a closer look at ourselves. The human perspective will always be deficient. Our sinful natures will always lean toward forgetting those three words, "God has promised." We see a low bank account, the absence of a job, the difficulty of a child, the challenge of an elderly parent, the car that won't start, or the sickness without a cure and it's easy to get discouraged, depressed, or distracted. Satan really doesn't care which one of those we experience—any of them will put us right where he wants us—focusing on the impossibilities and not on our all-things-are-possible God.

Something else we must not overlook is what happened when Israel demonstrated a lack of faith in God's promise. By pushing forward their own agenda, they dishonored God before nonbelievers. Those nations who had heard the stories of an all-powerful God, changed their perspective. He was not the God who saves, but weak and of no consequence.

The next time you face a personal mountain, remember *God has promised*. An impossible task becomes possible with Him. Nothing is too wide, too high, too long, or too deep for Jesus to do for us. Turn your mountains over to Him. And don't be surprised when those who witness your life, also see an Almighty God and are renewed.

An impossible task becomes possible with Him.

FURTHER READING

Patriarchs and Prophets, pages 374-392

The Story of Redemption, pages 158-163

The Bible Story, vol. 3, pages 13-31

Renew YOUR SPIRIT

make new • restore • replenish • reestablish • revive

DIGGING DEEPER

In 1961, Wayne Booth, a literary critic, introduced the idea of the "unreliable narrator." The unreliable narrator is a storyteller who can't be trusted. Typically the speaker leads the reader along, often as a trusted reporter. It's only towards the end of the story the reader discovers they've been misled.

> The unreliable narrator is a storyteller who cannot be trusted.

While Booth was primarily referencing fiction, in general, first person accounts of any event are "unreliable." This is because when one tells a story, the account is often influenced by the person's perspective and opinion. That's why in a court of law, you want more than one witness.

This becomes important to us because our lesson this week finds an unreliable narrator in the 10 spies that return to tell their story. Unreliable narrators have a variety of classifications, but the two that apply to Numbers 13 are the "exaggerator" and the "liar." As you might suspect, one overstates the facts to make them more impressive while the other outright deceives.

Read Numbers 13:27, 28 again. Note the word translated "nevertheless." In the original language this word suggests that it is impossible for man. By adding this word into their message to the people, they indicated their lack of faith as well as revealing their human perspective. Read the verse again without the word, "nevertheless," and notice how it changes the message. In this way they were simply reporting the facts. We went and we saw this. Adding "nevertheless" suggested that the task could not be accomplished and in so doing, discredited God as limited in His power to grant what He had promised since Abraham.

Now move down to verse 32. The phrase translated "they gave" in the original language means "to invent" or "to spread around." Ellen White in *Patriarchs and Prophets* (p. 388) reveals that the 10 spies relished the power their false report brought to the camp. They embellished it more and more and exaggerated the height of those living in Canaan, even reversing their original report. The land that was "flowing with milk and honey," now "devoured its inhabitants."

Turn your *mountains* over to Him.

MAKING IT REAL

The 10 spies left out the most essential part of their assignment—"God has promised." This week think about what God has promised you. Then each time you are tempted to be irritated, annoyed, challenged, restless, or angry, put the situation into perspective. **I will not be [fill in the blank] because God has promised [finish the sentence.]**

WEEK THIRTY-FOUR

Rebellion in the Wilderness

READ **NUMBERS 14:39-45; 16; 17**

Numbers 16:3 *They gathered together against Moses and Aaron, and said to them, "You take too much upon yourselves, for all the congregation is holy, every one of them, and the Lord is among them. Why then do you exalt yourselves above the assembly of the Lord?"*

RENEW YOUR MIND

I've always had an interest in the American Revolution. I'm not completely sure why it captures my attention, but it does, and thus I've done a bit of reading on the subject including the biography, *John Adams*, by David McCullough. He quotes Adams as saying:

"I've always been dissatisfied, I know that. But lately I find that I reek of discontentment. It fills my throat, and it floods my brain. And sometimes I fear there is no longer a dream, but only the discontentment."

Adams says this in the context of his dream of American independence from Britain. Of his own admission, he described himself as "obnoxious, suspected and unpopular," but continued to push his cause of independence forward. Now he is known as one of the Founding Fathers of America.

To be quite honest, I can relate in some ways to what Adams has said—not the unpopular, obnoxious personality, but dissatisfaction. At certain points in my life, I've known it to fill my soul as well. It starts as an irritation with a church member, colleague, or situation; leads to annoyance and on to frustration. Hopefully you can relate and I'm not alone with John Adams as the only two who have ever felt the challenges of discontentment.

Korah, the focus of our lesson this week, also was dissatisfied. He, too, went down the road toward frustration. As I pondered his story, one that ends badly, I was startled to recognize we had something in common. Are we the same or are we different?

Different. And here's why. To become frustrated isn't wrong. John Adams in frustration pushed forward a new idea—a new nation. Frustration can lead to creating something better, and the chances of success rise exponentially if one also turns to God. Next should come prayer to change the individual, the situation, or yourself. But in Korah's case, his next step was self-exaltation and the spreading of false information in order to gain followers for his cause. Ellen White describes Korah rejecting the light and darkening his mind (*Patriarchs and Prophets*, p. 404). Korah lost sight of God who was literally right outside his tent flap.

The other night I had to maneuver my way through the house to the kitchen. Without turning on a light I easily made it to my destination in complete darkness. I could see the shapes of pictures on the walls, furniture, and toys to avoid. It was when I got to the kitchen and had to get something from the cupboard I realized I couldn't see to get what I needed and had to turn on the light. The room was flooded with brightness and I suddenly realized I wasn't seeing as well as I thought. I had only believed that I could.

Our lives can be like that walk in the darkness. We gradually move farther and farther away from the light of God's presence until we think we're living as we should, when in actuality we are walking in darkness. The solution is found in a well-known chorus:

Turn your eyes upon Jesus; Look full in His wonderful face. And the things of earth will grow strangely dim; In the light of His glory and grace.

How is it with you, friend? Are you walking in the darkness or the light? ⓫

> We gradually move farther and farther away from the light of God's presence until we think we're living as we should, when in actuality we are walking in darkness.

FURTHER READING

Patriarchs and Prophets, pages 392-405

The Bible Story, vol. 3, pages 32-41

Renew YOUR SPIRIT

make new • restore • replenish • reestablish • revive

DIGGING DEEPER

Korah's experience is one that should be studied again and again. Two significantly important events—the Golden Calf and Korah and his followers—were serious threats to Israel. In the first, God was replaced, while in the second God was ignored.

> In the first, God was replaced, while in the second God was ignored.

"He who would confess Christ must have Christ abiding in him. He cannot communicate that which he has not received. . . . Men (women) may deny Christ by evil speaking, by foolish talking, by words that are untruthful or unkind. They may deny Him by shunning life's burdens, by the pursuit of sinful pleasure. They may deny Him by conforming to the world, by uncourteous behavior, by the love of their own opinions, by justifying self, by cherishing doubt, borrowing trouble, and dwelling in darkness. In all these ways they declare that Christ is not in them. And "whosoever shall deny Me before men," He says, "him will I also deny before My Father which is in heaven." (*The Desire of Ages*, p. 357)

MAKING IT REAL

This story is challenging to each of us because of Korah's spirit to stir others toward rebellion. Take the time this week to ask yourself some serious questions:

- Have I ever said things that **might influence another** to think wrongly of someone else?
- Have I ever been **turned against an individual** because someone told me something about them?
- If yes to either, **how can I protect my mind and heart** from such conversations?

Make "Turn Your Eyes Upon Jesus" your theme song this week. Sing it each morning and evening. **How does it change the way you see things?**

"Turn your eyes upon *Jesus.*"

WEEK THIRTY-FIVE

A Sad Mistake

READ **NUMBERS 20:1-21; 21:1-9**

Numbers 20:29 *Now when all the congregation saw that Aaron was dead, all the house of Israel mourned for Aaron thirty days.*

RENEW YOUR MIND

I worked alongside a colleague for about 20 years. For the last part of those years our offices were right next door to each other. We shared the workload, used each other as sounding boards, and those days when the office was particularly a hard place to be, we encouraged each other. About 18 months ago, he retired. His position was not filled, and so I soldier on alone, now carrying most of his assignments along with my own. I miss him greatly.

> At the designated place, Aaron lays down and cradled in Moses' arms, he falls asleep, to waken when Jesus calls his name.

The day has come for Aaron to die. Strange, in a way, that a death would be scheduled. While certainly an old man, he still had a pep in his step, a light in his eye, and the will to carry the burden he'd carried along with his brother, Moses, for the past 40 years. Together with his brother and his son, they walked the mountain path.

It must have been a solemn journey broken by a chuckle here and there. I imagine they couldn't help but recount their days of ministry together. They'd rest here and there along the rocky trail, tell a few stories, relate another memory, and then move on. At the designated place, Aaron lays down and cradled in Moses' arms, he falls asleep, to waken when Jesus calls his name.

I'm reminded of my mother's passing. We were a small family of two—me and her. We'd journeyed together for my entire life with mostly the good and sometimes the bad. One Wednesday she awoke with sniffles. By Sunday, I stood by her bed in ICU, saying my last goodbyes, telling her I loved her. And then she was gone. It was not a death announced, but one that crept in quietly, quickly, and completely unexpected. I have no regrets, but one. I didn't say, "I will miss you." And I do. Every day.

God gives us people to walk with. Twenty years is a long time to share the daily grind of the workplace. Sixty-plus years with a parent is a blessing. But when each left, while feeling abandoned, I was not alone. Jesus is my Friend and will walk my journey with me for as long as I shall live. On Him do I lean. On Him do I trust.

Have you experienced loss? A colleague, a spouse, a parent, a pet? The pain of separation is keenly felt, but it opens us to rely on our heavenly Friend. Turn to Him today. In Him you will be renewed.

FURTHER READING

Patriarchs and Prophets, pages 406-432

The Story of Redemption, pages 164-169

The Bible Story, vol. 3, pages 42-57

Renew YOUR SPIRIT

make new • restore • replenish • reestablish • revive

DIGGING DEEPER

Moses and Aaron were not to enter Canaan, because of the incident at the rock at Horeb. There are several lessons we can learn from this story, but here are two.

Their punishment seems unduly harsh until one realizes that it went beyond simply not following directions. The rock was a symbol of Christ. The waters that flowed from the rock in each place they camped was illustrative of Jesus as the source of all our needs. "As the life-giving waters flowed from the smitten rock, so from Christ, "smitten of God," "wounded for our transgressions," "bruised for our iniquities" (Isaiah 53:4,5), the stream of salvation flows for a lost race." (*Patriarchs and Prophets*, p. 411).

> **Because the rock symbolized Christ and His sacrifice for us, the rock was not to be hit a second time. To do so would be to sacrifice Him a second time.**

This was the second time that God would bring water forth from a rock. The first time Moses struck the rock once. The second time he was to speak to the rock. Because the rock symbolized Christ and His sacrifice for us, the rock was not to be hit a second time. To do so would be to sacrifice Jesus a second time. Jesus died once for all. From then on, we must only ask for our needs. By Moses striking the rock, he forever marred this life lesson God wished to teach His people.

One might wonder why then did the water flow from the rock? Moses did not do as he was instructed so it shouldn't have worked, right? We are not dealing with a magic spell where simply saying the right incantation makes something appear. This is the living God, a God who loves His people and will provide for their needs. God would not withhold something as vital as water from Israel. He can work through imperfect people. While we may think we are doing right, as Moses thought in that moment, in actuality what appears to work isn't the way God intends it. We must draw near to God and be open to His leading and direction to achieve what He longs us to receive.

We can *always rely* on our Heavenly Friend.

MAKING IT REAL

Moses and Aaron sinned at the rock at Horeb. Because of this they suffered the disappointment of not entering the very land they had purposed their life toward for the past 40 years. Think of a disappointment in your life, something that you had worked toward, tried to make happen, set your heart on, and for whatever reason, it was not meant to be. As you think back, how can you see God working either during that moment or since? **Did God have better plans for you that you discovered after your experience?**

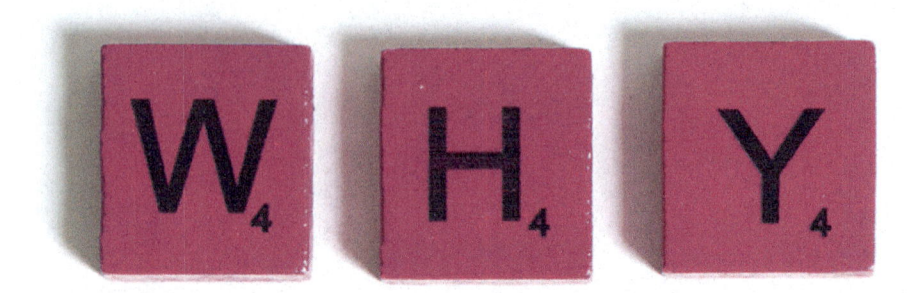

WEEK THIRTY-SIX

Balaam, the Greedy Prophet

READ **NUMBERS 21:21-25:18**

Numbers 24:17 *"I see Him, but not now; I behold Him, but not near; A Star shall come out of Jacob; A Scepter shall rise out of Israel."*

RENEW YOUR MIND

Back in Lesson 26, I introduced a TED Talk by promoter Simon Sinek. He developed three words—What, How, Why—into a marketing concept. He arranged them into a "Golden Circle," where the center circle is "why," the middle is "how," and the outer circle is "what." These three circles moving from the outside circle to the innermost circle represent Sinek's theory on how people think. First, they ask "What?" followed by "How?" and finally "Why?" Sinek's point is that inspiring leaders or organizations think, act, and communicate differently—that is, upside down or inside out. Successful leaders begin with "Why."

Sinek's point is that inspiring leaders or organizations think, act, and communicate differently—that is, upside down or inside out. Successful leaders begin with "Why."

Let's look at Balaam and Balak. Together they look at the "what," they develop the "how," but they never reason the "why." *What* they wanted to do was rid the earth of Israelites. *How* to do it, rested in cursing them. Never once do they wonder about "why" the Israelites are there in the first place. After Balak's frustration and Balaam's ambivalence, God gives Balaam one last prophecy and in it, He reveals the why: *I love them. I want to spend eternity with them. I have a plan.*

Applying this concept to God and spiritual things becomes an eye-opening experience. Throughout scripture, God, from a human perspective, is an upside-down communicator. Think about Jesus and His disciples. During most of His ministry, the disciples are scratching their heads. They'd ask a question (what or how) and He'd answer (why). Nicodemus asks Jesus what and how—Jesus answers why (John 3:16). The woman at the well asks what, Jesus answers why (John 4:26). On the road to Emmaus Jesus reveals the "why" throughout scripture—*I created you. I love you. I want to be with you forever.* The "how" is sending His Son to die for you. The "what" becomes easy—living with Him for eternity. The excited disciples run all the way back to Jerusalem. When you understand the "why," hearts and perspectives are transformed. Upside-down thinking changes the world.

When the Bible is read with an upside-down approach, it changes everything you might have thought about God. The "why" of God is found in Genesis through to Revelation. The message is about saving us because He loves us. And when we grasp that, we are moved to tell others and inspired to change the world. And, I might add, we are renewed.

FURTHER READING

Patriarchs and Prophets, pages 433-461

The Bible Story, vol. 3, pages 58-63

Renew YOUR SPIRIT

make new • restore • replenish • reestablish • revive

DIGGING DEEPER

Balaam seems an unlikely prophet for God to use in such a mighty way. His words of the coming Messiah echo down through history. "I see Him, but not now; I behold Him, but not near . . ." Balaam ended his life as a wicked man. It's because of Balaam that Israel commits another great sin before God (Num. 31:6). He returned to Moab and offered the suggestion to the king that the way to get Israel to sin was through sexual temptation. The men of Israel not only were seduced, but they also worshiped the gods of Moab. Later, Balaam was killed along with the kings of Midian (Num. 31:8) Balaam may be allowed to see Jesus whose coming he foretold, but if he does, it will not be in wonderful expectation, but in hopelessness and fear for he did not listen to the voice of God, but to the temptation of wealth, pride, and power.

> Balaam may be allowed to see Jesus whose coming he foretold, but if he does, it will not be in wonderful expectation, but in hopelessness and fear.

MAKING IT REAL

This idea of upside-down thinking takes a bit of time to grasp. Asking "why" isn't where we typically go first. As you read your Bible during your daily devotionals this week, practice applying this concept. Don't ask *what* God is saying or *how* He is saying it, ask yourself *why*. After you have figured out the answer, then follow with discovering the how and what. You will be amazed at how differently your Bible reads.

Upside-down thinking changes the world.

WEEK THIRTY-SEVEN

The Promised Land at Last

> **READ** **DEUTERONOMY 31-34; JOSHUA 1-4; 5:13-6:27**

Joshua 3:15, 16 *Those who bore the ark came to the Jordan, and the feet of the priests who bore the ark dipped in the edge of the water . . . that the waters which came down from upstream stood still, and rose in a heap.*

> **RENEW YOUR MIND**

We dropped my youngest daughter at the university for her junior year of college. Most of the summer she repeatedly told us she did not want to return to campus, but we encouraged her that it was going to be her best year yet. When we left, however, it was a tearful goodbye and a challenge to continue driving leaving her 500 miles away from home.

Always a child with natural intuition, but lacking the words to articulate her deeper feelings, she was right. The school year, only 48 hours old, wasn't going well. There were a number of tearful conversations until we finally said, "You can leave, but only to go to another college. You have two days to make up your

> A man from each tribe was to take a stone from the middle of the river to the other side. These 12 stones were stacked one on the other to serve as a reminder.

mind." While that sounds harsh it was the truth—other colleges were beginning and the more she delayed, the farther behind she would get. Completely torn in what to do, my next words to her were: "Sometimes you just have to put your foot in the water."

The reference, of course, was to our lesson this week. Go back and read Joshua 1:2. Note that God does not tell Joshua how he's supposed to get a nation of some two million people across the Jordan at flood stage. He just tells him to do it. Joshua doesn't hesitate. He prepares the people, and they walk toward the Jordan. There is no plan other than to follow the Ark (God). Imagine what the priests are thinking as they walk closer and closer to the Jordan. The first priest's toe touches the water—and suddenly it stops flowing. God prepared a way. They only had to follow Him.

While the people crossed, another instruction was given. A man from each tribe was to take a stone from the middle of the river to the other side. These 12 stones were stacked one on the other to serve as a reminder. When they passed by these stones and their children asked what they meant, it would serve as a prompt to tell them all God had done in the past, as well as a reminder that He would lead in the future.

My daughter has a "stone" in her collection marked junior year. She stepped out in faith, changed colleges, and for her, the "waters parted," and everything fell into place. What stones do you have? Have you pulled out your collection recently and taken a look? Where did God show up for you? Where did you put your foot out in faith and see the waters part? If you haven't looked recently, do it soon. Remind yourself and be renewed.

FURTHER READING

Patriarchs and Prophets, pages 462-493

The Story of Redemption, pages 170-181

The Bible Story, vol. 3, pages 67-91

Renew YOUR SPIRIT

make new • restore • replenish • reestablish • revive

DIGGING DEEPER

In our chapters this week, Moses dies. This venerable and faithful leader of Israel walks up the mountain alone. Moses is afforded a great privilege. God knew his desire to stay with his people and to see the Promised Land, and so God puts on one of the greatest "movies" rivaling anything man could produce. He allows Moses to see this great land of promise from one end of it to the other. He then shows the history of the Israelites through to the time of Jesus and to the end of the age with the Second Coming. I can imagine Moses' heart thrilling with all he saw as well as great wells of sadness as he witness the failure of his people, including the killing of God's Son. When it was done, Moses lays down and falls asleep awaiting the final trumpet call of his Savior.

Interestingly, the wait wasn't long because Christ Himself came to call Moses from the grave. All that Moses witnessed for the future, he has been able to watch "livestream" from his place in the heavenly kingdom.

A wonderful statement is given in *Patriarchs and Prophets*, p. 481. After reading this, you may look at sunsets with a bit more meaning:

"Moses was dead, but his influence did not die with him. It was to live on, reproducing itself in the hearts of his people. The memory of that holy, unselfish life would long be cherished, with silent, persuasive power molding the lives even of those who had neglected his living words. As the glow of the descending sun lights up the mountain peaks long after the sun itself has sunk behind the hills, so the works of the pure, the holy, and the good shed light upon the world long after the actors themselves have passed away. Their works, their words, their example, will forever live. "The righteous shall be in everlasting remembrance."

How can you live your life so that after you are gone, your life is like the lasting glow of a sunset?

God prepares a way.
We only have to *follow*.

MAKING IT REAL

Take the time to make a list of times when God was present in your life. It might be an answered prayer, an unexpected gift, a job offer, a marriage proposal, or any other number of things. These are your "stones." Keep the list in a place where you can occasionally review them. Add to them as God leads. Use them as encouragers for when things may not be going well.

If you have children, talk about the "stones" in your life at family worship. Each evening, tell them a different story about when God "parted the waters" for you. Help them to understand that God is also leading in their lives. Ask them about what "stones" they have experienced. Start their collection today.

WEEK THIRTY-EIGHT

Blessings and Curses

READ **DEUTERONOMY 27; 28; JOSHUA 7; 8**

Joshua 8:32 *And there, in the presence of the children of Israel, he wrote on the stones a copy of the law of Moses, which he had written.*

RENEW YOUR MIND

Author's Note: *These devotions were written well ahead of when they were posted on the website or, in this case, published. It continues to amaze me how often what God has inspired coincided exactly with the time they were released. This devotion was no exception. Even though written earlier, it was posted to the website right at the time of the passing of Queen Elizabeth II (September 8, 2022).*

In June 2022, those in the United Kingdom celebrated the Queen's Platinum Jubilee, the first time such an event has occurred in British history. Acknowledging her coronation each year was, for Queen Elizabeth II, an opportunity to remember the oath she took before God. It is something she did not take lightly. The Queen, almost to a fault, placed the British throne first. Her commitment was to God's calling, then her subjects, followed by everyone and everything else.

What the Israelites faced on the mountains of Ebal and Gerizim was not unlike what Queen Elizabeth II experienced at her coronation. Just as she was set aside to rule on His behalf, they were to covenant with God before crossing into the Promised Land. What differs is that this isn't Israel's first go at this. This was less like a coronation and much more like a marriage gone wrong.

A covenant service occurred at Sinai, a year after leaving Egypt. At that time, God Himself appeared in fire, thunder, lightning, and dark clouds. Israel agreed to do all that God commanded. They set themselves apart for the Lord, but it lasted only six short weeks. The covenant was broken when they built the golden calf and abandoned God. Subsequently, God required a renewing of their promise—a time of recommitment not unlike a married couple who breaks their vows through adultery and decides to stand again before the altar to renew their vows declaring to honor, love, and cherish.

You might think this mountain experience of declaration for God doesn't particularly relate to us today. Yet we do have a similar opportunity to renew our covenant with God. Within the Adventist Church that experience can be found each time we participate in the communion service. Full of symbolism, it serves as a reminder as well as a time of recommitment. We wash each other's feet in an act of humility, service, and reminder of baptism. We drink the juice, and eat the bread, remembering the amazing gift of salvation through Jesus' death on the cross. When we leave, we are reconsecrated in our service and commitment to God.

Think of this the next time there is a communion service. Don't shy away, become uncomfortable, or go through the motions. Savor and embrace it as an opportunity to rededicate to service, recommit to following God's plan, and most importantly, to be renewed.

> **Her commitment was to God's calling, then her subjects, followed by everyone and everything else.**

FURTHER READING

Patriarchs and Prophets, pages 493-504

The Bible Story, vol. 3, pages 92-95

Renew YOUR SPIRIT

make new • restore • replenish • reestablish • revive

DIGGING DEEPER

This story of Mount Gerizim (the mount of blessing) and Mount Ebal (the mount of cursing) is one that doesn't get told. It's one of those parts of the Bible often relegated to be forgotten. It's no one's favorite and preachers don't build their sermons around it. It did, however, come to the forefront in March 2022, when the announcement was made of a "curse tablet" found near Mount Ebal and part of a previously excavated site called "Joshua's altar."

> It is one of those parts of the Bible that is often relegated to be forgotten, not anyone's favorite. It isn't retold nor are sermons built around it.

An archaeologist decided to go through a dump site of what was discarded 30 years earlier using a different technique and found the small one inch square tablet with this inscription:

"Cursed, cursed, cursed — cursed by the God YHW. You will die cursed. Cursed you will surely die. Cursed by YHW – cursed, cursed, cursed."

The discovery has excited not only the archaeological community, but religious and biblical scholars as well. It places the name of Yahweh much earlier than once thought, and also gives supporting evidence to the biblical account.

It is a lesson to us about the Bible and its stories. What we might think unimportant, not worthy to study, may be to discard a "gem" into the trash heap. Read your Bible. Study it thoroughly. Pray and ponder each story no matter how insignificant. It may be that story that changes your life allowing you to see God more clearly than before.

MAKING IT REAL

This week is a good time to recommit yourself and your family to Jesus. Think of ways you might make this meaningful.

Recommit to following God's plan, and be *renewed*.

WEEK THIRTY-NINE

The Gibeonites

READ **JOSHUA 9; 10:1-15**

Joshua 9:3, 4 But when the inhabitants of Gibeon heard what Joshua had done to Jericho and Ai, they worked craftily, and went and pretended to be ambassadors.

RENEW YOUR MIND

Are you familiar with the term, "settle for less"? It can be used in relationships—don't settle for less when selecting a marriage partner. Business—don't settle for less than what you have paid for. Career—don't settle for a job that does not bring fulfillment and satisfaction. In other words, aim high—get what you deserve.

Now this is secular thinking for the most part, but interestingly we find it in our story today. *Patriarchs and Prophets* reveals that the Gibeonites were wealthy Hivites, living in a "royal city." They, along with other Canaanite cities, had heard of the story of Israel and their God. While the other cities galvanized toward war, the Gibeonites went to Israel to ask for a treaty. But instead of doing it honestly with full transparency, they settled for deception. And it worked. For three days that is. When Israel discovered the ruse, while they did not attack Gibeon, they did "curse" them by making them slaves to Israel forever, by forcing them to serve the sanctuary as woodcutters and water carriers.

Certainly, this is an example of living life honestly. But to simply stop there is to miss a greater point. In making a treaty with Israel, the Gibeonites pledged to honor and serve Israel's God. Israel was to conquer Canaan destroying all heathen nations, but there was an exception. The "stranger" who accepted God would be as "one born among you" (Lev. 19:33,34). The Gibeonites settled for less. Had they gone to Israel declaring their allegiance to God, they would have been accepted under the covenant with all the rights and privileges afforded Israel. In this, honesty really was the best policy.

The Gibeonites, though, accept the consequences of their actions with much humility. Once wealthy and "royal," they are now slaves. This is where we may miss the greater lesson—God's grace. Yes, the Gibeonites "settled." Yes, they were now slaves tasked with menial labor for the rest of their existence. But notice that where they were once "outsiders," they are now closer in their proximity to God then even the children of Israel themselves. The sanctuary was where God resided. To be cursed to serve God at the sanctuary was to draw them into an inner circle close to the very presence of God. God's grace was extended to those who did not come to Him in full understanding or trust.

What an amazing God we serve! We stumble through our lives. We don't trust in Him to provide for us. We don't consult Him in all we do. We make mistakes. We are careless in our connection mixing the sacred and the common. And yet He welcomes us, not at a distance, but draws us into His inner circle, close to Him, in complete love and forgiveness. How can we not be renewed?

> Where they were once "outsiders," they are now closer in their proximity to God then even the children of Israel themselves.

FURTHER READING

Patriarchs and Prophets, pages 505-509

The Bible Story, vol. 3, pages 96-101

Renew YOUR SPIRIT

make new • restore • replenish • reestablish • revive

DIGGING DEEPER

When one settles for less they accept a life with limitations instead of soaring as high as one might go experiencing all that God has in store. Several Christian preachers and commentators (David Jeremiah and others) have coined the phrase, "Peter Pan Christians." You may know the story of Peter who didn't want to grow up, staying a boy forever. And while there are some of us who would like to go back to our childhood because it was "easier," we know what we would miss out on if we had never matured.

> Several Christian preachers and commentators (David Jeremiah and others) have coined the phrase, "Peter Pan Christians." The idea of a "Peter Pan Christian," is one who does not grow in Christ, one who fails to mature.

The idea of a "Peter Pan Christian," is one who does not grow in Christ, one who fails to mature. The sermon on Sabbath is enough Bible study for the week. Watching the service online is easier than participating in the fellowship. Sleeping on Sabbath afternoons is the "rest" God offered at creation. While there is nothing wrong with a great sermon, remote services, or a good nap, to do this routinely is to miss out on what God has in store. We are to grow continually through Bible study, through service to others, and through being part of the fellowship of believers.

MAKING IT REAL

To settle is sometimes also a compromise. We become comfortable in what we are doing, not realizing that we might actually experience more. Think about what you do daily or weekly that allows you to grow in Christ. What could you do to make this experience even better? How could you adjust your day to allow more time in your Bible? In prayer? In praise?

Grow
with God.
Discover His plan
for you.

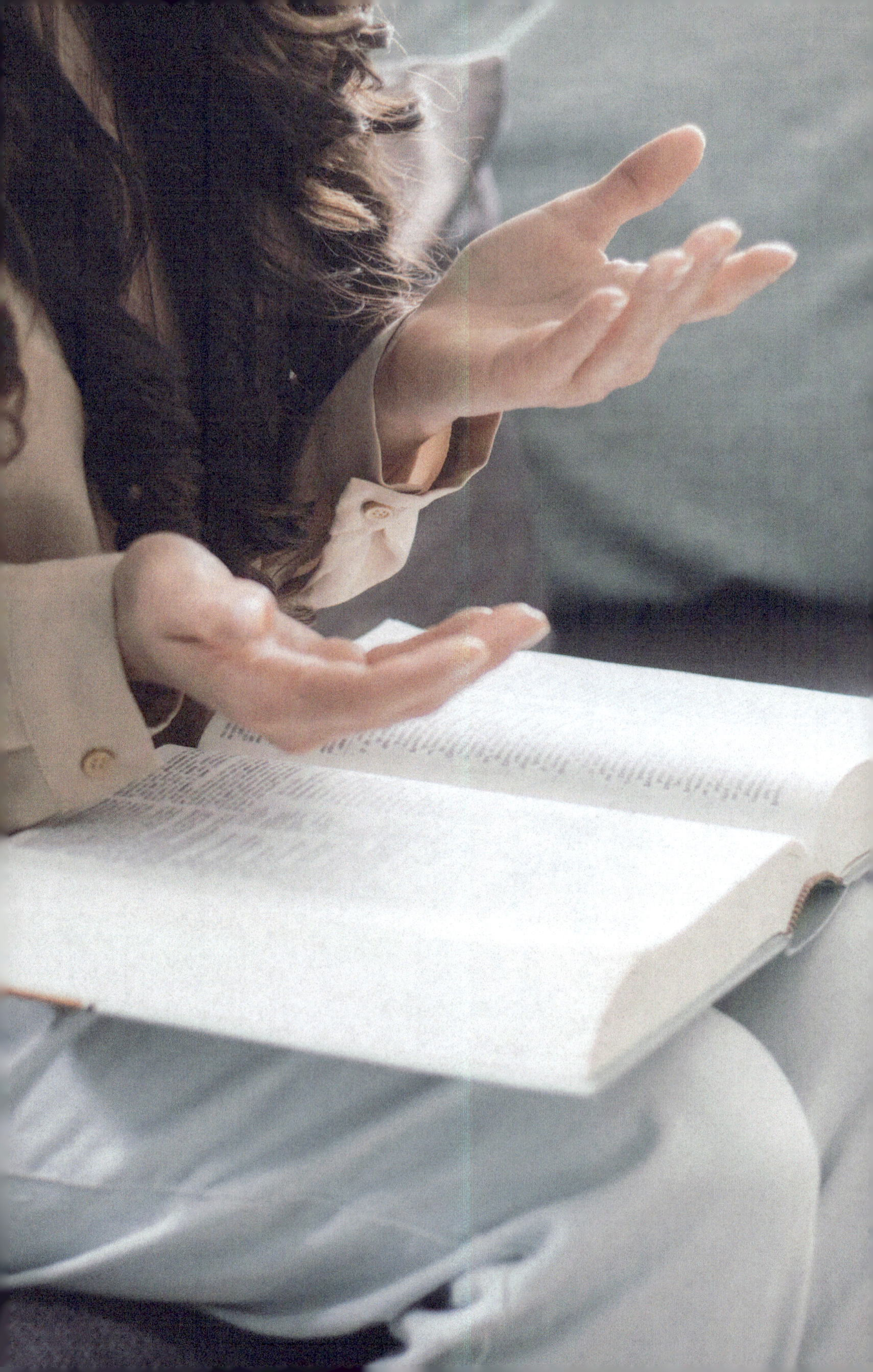

PART FOUR

Accepting His Call

WEEK FORTY

Up and Down Years

READ **JOSHUA 13-24; JUDGES 1-5**

Joshua 22:10 *And when they came to the region of the Jordan which is in the land of Canaan, the children of Reuben, the children of Gad, and half the tribe of Manasseh built an altar there by the Jordan—a great, impressive altar.*

RENEW YOUR MIND

There's a not-to-be-missed story found in the midst of the land appropriations by Joshua. There too many details to retell here completely, so if you have not read Joshua 22 and can stop now to read, do so and then return to this devotional.

For those who cannot, let me do a brief summary. The two-and-a-half tribes who decided to settle on the east side of the Jordan were returning after doing their part to conquer Canaan. As they approached the Jordan they decided to erect an exact replica of the altar found at the Tabernacle. Word got back to the tribes on the west side of the Jordan and things went awry from there.

There are a number of important lessons on both sides to glean from this story, and thus why it shouldn't be overlooked.

1. **Be transparent.** While the Eastern tribes meant no harm, they weren't transparent with their plans. This caused no end of grief and anger that could have been avoided. A simple lesson, but an important one. Let

people know what you are planning, and why it is important.
2. **Listen carefully and respond calmly when falsely accused.** This can be so hard! The immediate response is to get defensive, interrupt, cry, become angry, or a combination of all four. The Eastern tribes listened first, then responded. True active listening will make a difference in your encounters with others, no matter how challenging they are.
3. **Don't jump to conclusions.** The Western tribes were guilty of this in a big way. When they heard of the duplicate altar, they declared war! Fortunately, cooler heads prevailed. A delegation went to investigate, but even their words were harsh and unkind. Be careful that what you see is really what is there.
4. **If you're in the wrong, acknowledge your mistake.** This is, perhaps, the most difficult—admitting you were wrong. It can make the biggest difference in your relationships. Sometimes we're wrong and need to apologize for our actions. The Western tribes were wrong. They didn't apologize but did leave satisfied with the explanation.
5. **It's good to be vigilant for God but be careful of extremes.** The Israelite leaders were reacting strongly because they remembered their past. They specifically mentioned past events that led to serious consequences and punishment by God. Their hearts were in the right place, but in the end, they misrepresented God by their words and behavior. Absolutely guard and defend God, His Word, His prophets, and His commandments. Stand firm. But choose your words carefully and lovingly.

As parents, employees, managers, or leaders, we will be confronted by people (or children) who appear to be in the wrong. It's easy to judge motives and jump to conclusions. And we may often be more right than wrong as we do so. But ponder how to best represent God to others, while holding firm to what you believe. When we do we will be renewed in our relationship with others.

> As parents, employees, managers, leaders, we will be confronted with people (children) who appear to be doing something wrong. It is easy to judge motives and jump to conclusions.

FURTHER READING

Patriarchs and Prophets, pages 510-545

The Story of Redemption, pages 181-182

The Bible Story, vol. 3, pages 102-113

Renew YOUR SPIRIT

make new • restore • replenish • reestablish • revive

DIGGING DEEPER

As part of dividing the land in Canaan, Joshua set apart six cities as "cities of refuge." While they may not hold the same meaning today, they carried important symbolism.

> "No power can take out of His hands the souls that go to Him for pardon."

"The cities of refuge appointed for God's ancient people were a symbol of the refuge provided in Christ. The same merciful Saviour who appointed those temporal cities of refuge has by the shedding of His own blood provided for the transgressors of God's law a sure retreat, into which they may flee for safety from the second death. No power can take out of His hands the souls that go to Him for pardon. 'There is therefore now no condemnation to them which are in Christ Jesus.' 'Who is he that condemneth? It is Christ that died, yea rather, that is risen again, who is even at the right hand of God, who also maketh intercession for us;' that 'we might have a strong consolation, who have fled for refuge to lay hold upon the hope set before us.' Romans 8:1, 34; Hebrews 6:18." (*Patriarchs and Prophets*, p. 516)

MAKING IT REAL

The last part of Joshua 24:15 is one we know from memory: "But as for me and my house, we will serve the Lord." Whether you're an adult or have children, find some paper, crayons, markers, glitter, and anything else to encourage creativity.

If your children can write or copy, have them write this verse on their paper. Then have them decorate it. When they are done, hang their drawing near a door of your house. If you have more than one child, use various doors—the front, back, or the bathroom. Leave them there so that each time you come in and each time you leave the family is reminded—we serve Jesus.

We did this in our home when our girls were small. They are now young adults, and we only took down their artwork a few years ago when we replaced it with a wooden etching that now hangs over the doorframe. This activity blessed our home for a long time, and it will do the same for yours.

As for me and
my house, we will

serve the Lord.

WEEK FORTY-ONE

The Call of Gideon

READ **JUDGES 6**

Judges 6:12 *And the Angel of the Lord appeared to him, and said to him, "The Lord is with you, you mighty man of valor!"*

RENEW YOUR MIND

I don't know where you are in your life right now. Most reading these devotionals are probably young parents for that is the purpose of these lessons. But I'm guessing there are also those who are yet to be parents as well as those whose parenting is never completed, but the children have left the "nest." I'm in this category and actually edging closer to retirement. As I do, I've noticed my prayers changing a bit.

For me the future seems uncertain. Before when children entered our home, their lives dictated our lives. We were involved in what seemed a never-ending cycle of caring, educating, entertaining, and more as they grew. Where would they go to school turned into where would they go to high school to where would they go to college to where would they work to who they would marry. Now that they are safely on their own and blessed in their own rights, our lives are more open, more free, and to be honest, a bit more scary.

That's why reading Gideon's story is a blessing. Gideon was simply surviving. Maybe his prayers were similar to mine. Not that I'm suffering by any means, but no matter what causes the uncertainty, our prayers can be similar. The hope for me comes from two things that happened next in his story.

First, an Angel shows up. He comes when least expected. In fact, isn't that typical? We pray and pray for God to reveal, do, or change something, and then when He answers, we're often surprised. Lesson to me (and all of us), be ready for God to show up, because He will.

Second, notice the greeting given to Gideon: "The Lord is with you, you mighty man of valor!" (Judges 6:12, NKJV). It's the second part that intrigues me most. Notice that the Lord calls him what he *will be*. There's no indication that Gideon had done anything of any significance to earn such a greeting. But God was calling him to a job that, with God's help, he would become.

I don't know where I will be in the next three years or what I will be doing. I doubt I will be conquering Midianites, but I know I want to be alert, listening, and open to God saying to me: "The Lord is with you, you mighty woman of . . .!" I want to serve Him. I want to do what He calls me to do. I want to be what He sees I will become. I will rest in His will and be renewed.

> First, an Angel shows up. He comes when least expected. In fact, isn't that typical?

FURTHER READING

Patriarchs and Prophets, pages 545-548

The Bible Story, vol. 3, pages 115-120

Renew YOUR SPIRIT

make new • restore • replenish • reestablish • revive

DIGGING DEEPER

Although God saw and recognized Gideon's potential where he was, it didn't immediately alter Gideon's thoughts of himself. Notice the six times Gideon's words reveal his resistance to what God is calling him to do.

> Fear is something that can easily prevent us from following through on God's call.

1. "If the Lord is with us, why then has all this happened to us?" (v. 13). We pray and when God answers or provides a solution, we often begin to question instead of accepting, praising, and thanking Him. Be open to His voice and response.
2. "I *am* the least in my father's house." (v. 15). How often do we immediately focus on what we lack. No one will listen. No one will be interested. No one will answer the door. No one will pay attention. With God we are never "least."
3. "If now I have found favor in Your sight, then show me a sign . . ." (v. 17). Another typical response we share with Gideon. When God calls, do not doubt. Rise up and go in faith of His promises.
4. "But because he feared his father's household and the men of the city . . ." (v. 27) Fear is something that can easily prevent us from following through on God's call. We are afraid of what people might think, that we might fail, or that people will criticize. When God calls, He will protect and defend us.
5. "If You will save Israel by my hand as You have said—" (v. 36, 39). Gideon struggled with letting go of doubt and fear. God was ever-patient with him and provided him the answer to not one test, but two! God is aware of our humanness, our doubts, our fears, but steps up to help us.

I don't know if Gideon expected to be called to be a warrior. God may call you to do something you completely do not expect. Be open. Be unafraid. Trust in God.

Be ready for God
to show up, because

He will.

MAKING IT REAL

Wondering what God will provide in the future is challenging when you focus only on that. The best thing to do is exactly what the Israelites did repeatedly—remember the past. Why not make a list at evening worship of everything God has done for you or your family in the past? You might be surprised at how long the list is, and if God can do all of that for you, certainly He will do the same and more in the future.

WEEK FORTY-TWO

"Little" Tests

READ **JUDGES 7**

Judges 7:7 *Then the Lord said to Gideon, "By the three hundred men who lapped I will save you, and deliver the Midianites into your hand. Let all the other people go, every man to his place."*

RENEW YOUR MIND

I know of an organization where there have been a myriad of challenges. COVID played a part, as did layoffs, new personnel, financial issues, and more. It's not surprising then that morale might be somewhat low. There appears to be an attempt to rebuild, reorganize, and restructure. Whether the attempt will succeed or fail will depend on many things, not the least of which are the employees themselves.

I recently was made aware of a conversation between some of those employees. One, in particular, was extremely negative—recounting all the past challenges, poor hires, and poor decisions, essentially expressing a lack of confidence in leadership to fix any of it. While we may understand and even have experienced something like this ourselves, it made me wonder if this might be the kind of individual that God was "sorting" from Gideon's army.

It seems a peculiar strategy when one believes that quantity wins. The more soldiers or people or votes, the better chance for victory. But God's perspective is entirely different. He sorts out the fearful, the faithless, and the false. I'm sure Gideon was alarmed when 31,700 of his men were dismissed by God and he was left with a mere 300.

But a greater point remains. This story demonstrates that even one person deficient in their confidence and faith in God can influence others whether it is in a family, a church, or an organization. A small group confident in God's leading will always be more successful.

Sometimes it's hard to let people go. Sometimes it's hard to see people quit or walk away angry. But losing that individual may be exactly what is needed to arrive at the place God has planned. The point is not that smaller groups are more effective than larger ones, but that the influence of one individual may be the very thing keeping the fulfillment of God's plan possible.

First, a hard question. Are you someone who is keeping God's plan from moving forward? If the Holy Spirit leads you to answer yes, how can you be more of a facilitator than a deterrent?

Or are you the "Gideon" God has called to lead a small group of believers? Pray about God's plan. Let Him guide your heart and mind. If convicted, don't be deterred from listening to the Holy Spirit's call if large numbers of people won't join the effort. If people scorn, delay, ask for more research, surveys, or outside experts, listen, but weigh it against what God has said in His Word. It may mean going forth alone or with a few because God can and will bless and make a difference. Be strong. Be of good courage. Be renewed.

A small group confident in God's leading will always be more successful.

FURTHER READING

Patriarchs and Prophets, pages 548-559

The Bible Story, vol. 3, pages 121-123

Renew YOUR SPIRIT

make new • restore • replenish • reestablish • revive

DIGGING DEEPER

There is another takeaway from this story that involves fear and the ability to trust in God.

Between Judges 6 and 7, we find a fearful Gideon. He asks for a sign and it is given. The sign is enough for him to feel confident to tear down an altar, but only enough. He asks for a second sign involving the fleece. God answers this request, but this time the sign doesn't even last a few minutes before Gideon asks for a third sign—the reverse of his previous one. God obliges and assures that, yes, He will be with Gideon.

> When God wants to use us, no matter the circumstances, He will remove all obstacles. We only need to believe and follow.

Gideon gathers his forces, but God steps in and winnows them down. Gideon's confidence begins to waver as he sees thousands leaving his command. Now God steps in *and creates a sign of His own*—if Gideon will go down to the Midianite camp, he'll be encouraged. Gideon does, and coincidentally finds himself at just the right tent at just the right time to hear two Midianites say exactly what God has said from the beginning! Gideon didn't seem to find confidence in God's words, but he does from two unbelievers!

Our fears are no match for God's leading. When God wants to use us, no matter the circumstances, He will remove all obstacles. We only need to believe and follow.

MAKING IT REAL

Is God calling you to serve? Maybe we are doubtful of our ability. Perhaps we've never given a Bible study before. Our voice might not be what we think the choir needs. We've never thought we were great with children. It doesn't take much to talk ourselves out of something God is impressing on our hearts.

Make a list of what you might do for God. Start to pray upon that list. Open your heart and mind to listen to His voice. Then with bold assurance go forth and do His bidding.

Our fears are
no match for
God's leading.

WEEK FORTY-THREE

Samson

READ **JUDGES 13-16**

Judges 16:17 *He told her all his heart, and said to her, "No razor has ever come upon my head, for I have been a Nazarite to God from my mother's womb. If I am shaven, then my strength will leave me, and I shall become weak, and be like any other man."*

RENEW YOUR MIND

I remember scrolling through Instagram one day and seeing a photo someone posted of their "perfectly" decorated dining room. I will admit, it was gorgeous. The picture led you to believe that this home was right out of a magazine. But if you looked carefully, there was a mirror on the wall of the dining room. What the poster didn't realize is that the mirror revealed a not-so-perfect-out-of-date-in-need-of-remodeling kitchen. Their home wasn't perfect! But the person would lead you to believe it was.

Samson was another sort of poser. He was a Nazarite—set apart for God. This meant he was to stay away from vineyard products—grapes, raisins, or wine; drink no intoxicating drink; never cut his hair, and avoid contact with a dead body. All of these were visible demonstrations of his devotion to God. I call him a poser because he lived his life a bit like the Instagram poster, at least where his hair was concerned. While he wasn't very good at keeping his vow, he didn't cut his hair. To all those looking at him, Samson was devoted to God. His amazing strength would suggest the same.

Yet when his hair was cut, it was a bit like looking into that mirror of the "perfect" dining room picture. Samson lost his strength, not because of his hair, but because of his heart. What seemed like a man devoted to God on the outside, was really an empty vessel in need of true conversion.

In captivity, Samson had the time to review his life, legacy, and loyalty. His choices, seen in the light of his circumstances, were not what they should have been. The once mighty man of strength had nowhere to turn except to the God he had treated thoughtlessly. Samson's heart changed. When his hair grew back, it now represented what was "real" on the outside *and* the inside. This time the sign of devotion was accompanied by a changed heart.

It is tempting to let people see only the beautiful parts of our lives, the perfect images that suggest we are something we may not always be. What is more important is our connection to God as well as how others see Him in us. Those are the moments to capture. Those are the moments to share. It's in complete devotion to Him that we find we are renewed. (Make sure you read Digging Deeper for a completely different perspective on Samson.) ®

What seemed like a man devoted to God on the outside, was really an empty vessel in need of true conversion.

FURTHER READING

Patriarchs and Prophets, pages 560-568

The Bible Story, vol. 3, pages 130-136

Renew YOUR SPIRIT

make new • restore • replenish • reestablish • revive

DIGGING DEEPER

There are several opinions about Samson. The redemptive view was mentioned in the devotional.

What sways people toward this view is Hebrews 11. There Samson is catalogued into one of the most important groups in the Bible, the "Hall of Faith." These individuals kept or demonstrated faith in such a way that they are considered remarkable followers of Jesus. It would be easy to conclude that Samson, since he is included, must have turned his life around at the end. But not so fast.

> If you study Samson's life, one discovers he was completely self-centered including his last prayer.

Ellen White does not comment specifically other than to say a life afforded such amazing gifts from God since conception as Samson's was, was lived about as poorly as possible. She goes on to say that his life ended under ignominious circumstances, although Samson did accomplish in death what he was commissioned to do in his life.

Another commentator makes two points.* First, if you study Samson's life, one discovers he was completely self-centered including his last recorded prayer. The prayer starts well but ends focused on avenging the Philistines for what was done to *him*—not to Israel, not to God, but to Samson.

Second, if you study Hebrews 11:32, Samson is mentioned, but not like the others. The last six are in pairs: first, Gideon and Barak, both with similar life choices; then Samson and Jephthah, both similar in their foolishness; and David and Samuel, who lead, for the most part, exemplary lives for God. It could be concluded that the preacher in Hebrews wasn't citing Samson as an amazing person who turned his life around but simply throwing him into his sermon. To speculate about Samson's change of heart simply because he's in this list would be to ignore all that is known of him. Thus, the commentator concludes that Samson is thinking only of revenge as he ground the grain, not that he recognized that he failed God.

Study Samson's life. We do not know the ultimate fate of Samson, but we know we must live our lives for God, making wise choices that please Him with the gifts He gives.

*K. Lawson Younger Jr., *Judges/Ruth*, The NIV Application Commentary, Zondervan, Grand Rapids, Michigan, USA, p. 326.

How do others *see Him* in us?

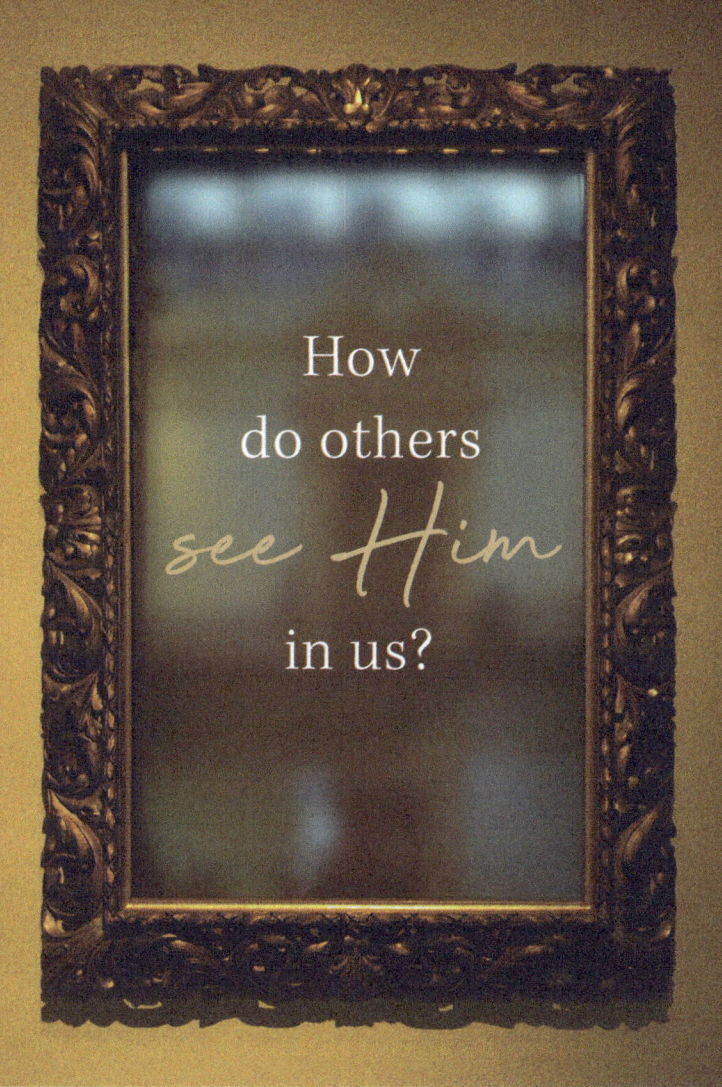

MAKING IT REAL

We shouldn't overlook Samson's parents, who eagerly desired to know how to care for this amazing gift from God. The instructions given to his mother would be some of the earliest known neonatal counsel. It is a reminder of the great responsibility we have for our children. This week:

- **If you are a parent,** think of the kind of things you are doing to grow your child spiritually. How do they see Jesus in you?
- **If you are a parent of grown children,** continue to place them before God. Be available. Be ready when they ask for help. Demonstrate Jesus to them.
- **If you are not a parent,** you're a mother (or father) in Israel. Pray for the children's programming at church. Engage your nieces or nephews. Find ways to be kind to neighborhood children. You may be the only way they see Jesus.

WEEK FORTY-FOUR

Faithful Ruth

READ **RUTH 1-4**

Ruth 4:16 *Then Naomi took the child and laid him on her bosom, and became a nurse to him.*

RENEW YOUR MIND

Recently my daughter shared a picture of her husband's grandparents surrounded by 13 of their 18 great-grandchildren, while holding up a onesie with the name of great-grandchild number 19 to be born in about a month. Eighteen plus great-grandchildren! What a blessing! But it reminded me of some who either have yet to become a grandparent or who have grandchildren and because of life's circumstances cannot see them or cannot have a meaningful relationship with them.

Allow me to venture off my usual purpose of writing to young parents, to concentrate for a few moments on more mature women. It is appropriate because the book of Ruth speaks to both generations—women who would be grandmothers, but also to those who suffer from infertility. That may come as a surprise to you as it did to me.

As I restudied this story, I caught something I had not seen before. Ruth 1:4 says that Mahlon and Kilion, Naomi's sons, married Moabite women—Orpah and Ruth. The story reveals that 10 years later both sons died. Here's what I'd not seen before—Naomi, who had already lost her husband, now lost two sons. *But* she also lost potential grandchildren. Interestingly, these two young women, married for 10 years, had failed to produce any children. Naomi's grief is threefold—her spouse, her sons, and their potential children.

I sympathize with this more because I'm a grandmother. Young women often long to become mothers. When older, the feeling transforms into the desire to become a grandmother. I'm blessed by the two boys that call me Grammie, but I have friends that don't yet have that privilege. More and more today, adult children are making choices that result in no grandchildren. While many women may not admit it, it's a loss they grieve.

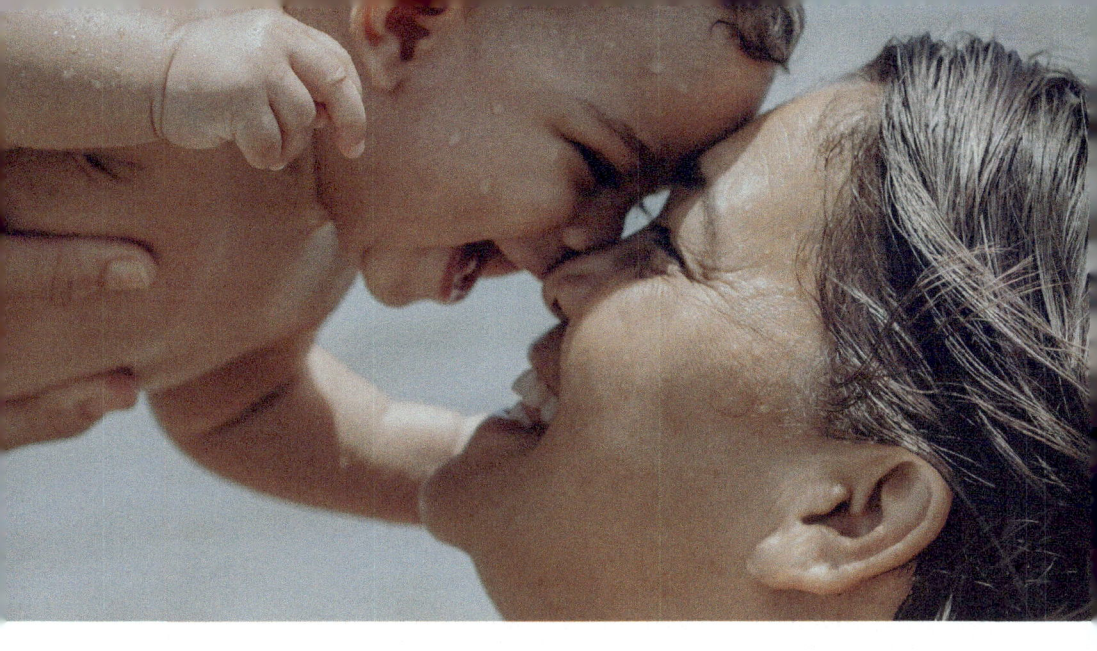

We should pause to also recognize infertility. It would appear that Ruth suffered from this. Perhaps she, too, longed for a child but was never able to conceive. As Naomi lost her son, and Ruth her husband, both grieve for what could have been.

God is mentioned twice in Ruth. In both, He offered aid—first He supplied grain for Bethlehem (Ruth 1:6) and at the end of the book enabled Ruth to become pregnant (4:13). Her infertility is relieved; she conceived and bore a son. And Naomi received her grandson, although they were not directly related.

I can see at least two lessons: First, God has a plan. Even in disappointment, there is a God who comforts and provides. The timing may not be ours, but the timing is always right.

Second, babies don't have to come from within your own family. Children need to be raised for the Lord no matter if they are related or not. If you deeply desire grandchildren and there doesn't seem to be one forthcoming, find a mother who will appreciate your help: volunteer in the beginner's Sabbath School or sit next to young parents in church prepared to entertain. And be patient. God has a plan for you and for your children. Allow Him to provide in His time and be content. Remember, relying on God for all that He can provide is how we are renewed.

> Even in disappointment, there is a God who comforts and provides. The timing may not be ours, but the timing is always right.

FURTHER READING

The Bible Story, vol. 3, pages 137-142

Renew YOUR SPIRIT

make new • restore • replenish • reestablish • revive

DIGGING DEEPER

To gain full meaning of the book of Ruth requires understanding a biblical concept that doesn't translate well from Hebrew to English. The word *hesed* (pronounced hes-ed) is found about 250 times in the Old Testament—three times in Ruth. When it's translated into English, it carries so much meaning that it translates into many different words. One might read *hesed* as mercy, compassion, love, loving-kindness, grace, or faithfulness.

> The word *hesed* is found about 250 times in the Old Testament.

Hesed describes relationships both between God and mankind or between humans. It isn't simply being kind, but when a person recognizes and acts to relieve an essential need of another, typically between a more powerful person toward a weaker person. *Hesed* is also voluntary; it's not mandatory or required.

Hesed is a characteristic of God. He (the more powerful) died for us (the weaker) so that we might have life (action) and He did it voluntarily. God grants us *hesed*.

For an example of *hesed* between humans, revisit the relationship between Jonathan and David.

MAKING IT REAL

Read the book of Ruth carefully this week as part of your individual or family worship—one chapter each day. As you do, identify where *hesed* is found in the book, whether explicit or implied. It might be divine-to-human (meaning God to an individual or group) or human-to-human, occurring between two people.

For example, an implied use of *hesed* is when God granted Ruth the ability to conceive and bear a child. There are three texts where the actual word is used: Ruth 1:8, 2:20, 3:10. **When you read those verses, what *hesed* is present? Divine-human or human-human?**

The timing may
not be ours,
but the timing is
always right.

WEEK FORTY-FIVE

Hannah's Prayer Answered

READ **1 SAMUEL 1; 2:1-11, 18-21**

1 Samuel 1:10 And she was in bitterness of soul, and prayed to the Lord and wept in anguish.

RENEW YOUR MIND

When your kids grow up and move out of your house they leave their stuff behind. When they purchase their own homes there comes a time when you start clearing out. Part of that process involves loading up your car, driving to their house, and unloading it despite their protests.

My youngest daughter was the recipient of one of those visits from her dad. Recently she decided to rummage through one of those boxes. In it she found her prayer journal from middle school. It was like a secret diary, but in this case her thoughts to God. From her now adult perspective, she smiled at her childish prayers, some of which included what I will call bargains—if You (God) do this for me, I'll do that for You.

This is where we find Hannah. Her level of desperation is such that she throws herself on her knees before God, and through sobs, silently mouths her prayer:

God, give me a son. If you do, I will give him back to You for the rest of his life.

Have you ever prayed a "bargain" prayer? Do this and I'll do that? Some call those "foxhole prayers" since they often arise during a crisis where there is little relationship with God or religion. *Save me! If You do, then I will . . .*

My daughter wasn't a foxhole pray-er, nor was Hannah. In both, they were leaning into the only One they knew could save them from their circumstances. For years, Hannah had silently endured the agony of infertility, and the disgrace, as well as the derision from the second wife. Now at the end of her limit, she opened herself up to a new approach to God that allowed God to work with her.

Hannah's offer is interesting. Any son she would bear would be a Levite as her husband was from the Levitical line (1 Chron. 6:33-38). Thus, her son would belong to God already from ages 30-50 (Num. 4:3; Num. 8:25). Hannah simply raised the stakes: "Let me have him for a few years and you can have him for the rest." And it explains Hannah's reasoning when Samuel was born not to return to the Sanctuary until the appointed time that she had agreed upon. Those first years were Hannah's alone. Then she held up her side of the bargain—Samuel was given to God for all time with her full support.

Prayer is a powerful tool no matter your age when trust is placed in God alone. Ellen White writes: "An appeal to heaven by the humble saint is more to be dreaded by Satan than the decrees of cabinets or the mandates of Kings" (*Signs of the Times*, Oct. 27, 1881).

Hannah's prayer was about resolving her desire to become a mother, but like the five loaves and two fish brought to Jesus, God multiplied her prayer. Not only did her son become the first prophet in Israel, but Samuel became pivotal in bringing Israel back to God. Hannah gave birth five more times after Samuel. Her bargain with God, her faithful commitment to her promise to Him, allowed Him to give back abundantly to her.

God listens. God cares. He's looking for ways to work with us. And in that we are renewed.

> **For years, Hannah had silently endured the agony of infertility, and the disgrace, as well as the derision from the second wife.**

FURTHER READING

Patriarchs and Prophets, pages 569-574

The Bible Story, vol. 3, pages 145-148

Renew YOUR SPIRIT

make new • restore • replenish • reestablish • revive

DIGGING DEEPER

One commentator reminds us:

"Birth narratives play an important role in biblical literature. They generally have specific features, all of which are present in Samuel's birth narrative. (1) The birth of the child marks a turning point, or at least some significant episode in Israel's history. (2) The narratives usually reveal something of the baby's character or future role in Israel's history. (3) Individuals whose births are announced in such a way are the solution to a dire problem. (4) Finally, such birth narratives always emphasize the providential significance of the new character's name."*

Those who have birth narratives in the Bible are: Isaac, Moses, Samson, Samuel, John, and Jesus.

> "Birth narratives play an important role in biblical literature. They generally have specific features, all of which are present in Samuel's birth narrative."

*Bill T. Arnold, *1 and 2 Samuel*, The NIV Application Commentary, Zondervan, Grand Rapids, Michigan, USA, p. 57.

MAKING IT REAL

Using the features listed above in Digging Deeper, look at each baby listed below and identify their four characteristics.

Isaac
Moses
Samson
Samuel
John
Jesus

God listens.

God cares.

WEEK FORTY-SIX

Samuel Hears God's Call

READ 1 SAMUEL 2:12-3:21

1 Samuel 3:10 Now the Lord came and stood and called as at other times, "Samuel! Samuel!" And Samuel answered, "Speak, for Your servant hears."

RENEW YOUR MIND

The midnight call to Samuel is a favorite story. One can easily picture the young boy eagerly obeying the elderly man, only to find out that it isn't Eli calling his name, but God. Consider these four important takeaways:

My oldest daughter attended an Adventist college. What wasn't known at the time, but discovered by the end of the year, was that the college chaplain had left, and they were still searching for a replacement. There was little spiritual leadership on the campus for that year, and it showed. What we had thought would be a great Adventist experience, was not. A bit disillusioned, she left for another Adventist school. Interestingly that first college is now thriving—it was simply an off year. But I never forgot the importance of spiritual leadership whether on a school campus, in a church, home, or office. Israel also learned this lesson when Eli was spiritually absent in his role as High Priest.

One can't read Samuel 3 without recognizing "the call" and then wondering how it applies to our life. All of us are called at some point by God, but it may take several times as it did with Samuel, and it may take time to recognize the Voice. What I find most intriguing is when there isn't a call. Is it possible that one doesn't get called? I'm reminded of the words from the hymn, "Live Out Thy Life Within Me," (#316, *Seventh-day Adventist Hymnal*) that references members who are "ready to have Thee use them or not be used at all." Being called can be scary, but not being called can also be challenging.

The Bible records that Samuel does not "know God yet" when the call arrives. This makes an interesting point for all of us. God knows each of us intimately—our very hairs are numbered. But we often don't know God. Our daily experience and relationship with God is all about discovering Him in our lives. Thus, listening intently for where we are needed, praying for direction, and resting contentedly in His plans is all part of "knowing God" and learning more about Him.

Last, in the story, Eli is the superior spiritual leader and Samuel is the child who has been lent to God for Eli to mentor and teach. Eli is the older, wiser, more experienced Christian. Samuel is the younger, less practiced, first learning of spiritual things. By the end of this story, things have shifted. Samuel, even in his youth, is called directly by God. God doesn't call Eli, but the inexperienced child. A time comes when the more experienced must give way to the younger less experienced. God has a need for them and a place, but it often means that the more mature must recognize their time of service has ended or lessened and allow others to take the lead.

Practice these four lessons: the importance of spiritual leadership; listening for the call, but content if there is none; learning of God each day through our daily walk with Him; and mentoring youth but knowing when to relinquish leadership to them. These are and will be challenging, but I promise, if practiced, you will find strength and be renewed.

It often means the more mature must recognize their time of service has ended or lessened and they must allow others to take the lead.

FURTHER READING

Patriarchs and Prophets, pages 575-582

The Story of Redemption, pages 183-185

The Bible Story, vol. 3, pages 149-154

Renew YOUR SPIRIT

make new • restore • replenish • reestablish • revive

DIGGING DEEPER

An unfortunate element in this story is Eli and his sons, Hophni and Phinehas, priests of Israel. We learn the sons aren't following God's ways, but their own. Ellen White, in *Patriarchs and Prophets*, gives some very serious counsel regarding the raising of children for God:

> Eli did not manage his household according to God's rules for family government.

"Those who follow their own inclination, in blind affection for their children, indulging them in the gratification of their selfish desires, and do not bring to bear the authority of God to rebuke sin and correct evil, make it manifest that they are honoring their wicked children more than they honor God. They are more anxious to shield their reputation than to glorify God; more desirous to please their children than to please the Lord and to keep His service from every appearance of evil" (p. 578).

"Eli did not manage his household according to God's rules for family government. He followed his own judgment. The fond father overlooked the faults and sins of his sons in their childhood, flattering himself that after a time they would outgrow their evil tendencies. Many are now making a similar mistake. They think they know a better way of training their children than that which God has given in His word. They foster wrong tendencies in them, urging as an excuse, 'They are too young to be punished. Wait till they become older and can be reasoned with.' Thus, wrong habits are left to strengthen until they become second nature. The children grow up without restraint, with traits of character that are a lifelong curse to them and are liable to be reproduced in others" (p. 578).

MAKING IT REAL

Knowing God is key in hearing or answering His call. Make a list of the characteristics you know about God. **What experiences in your walk with Him have helped you to learn these traits?**

Listen
for the call.

WEEK FORTY-SEVEN

Angels Guard God's Ark

READ **1 SAMUEL 4-6**

1 Samuel 4:5 *And when the ark of the covenant of the Lord came into the camp, all Israel shouted so loudly that the earth shook.*

RENEW YOUR MIND

Saying God is there doesn't make it so.
Eli, while he knew God and loved Him, didn't place God first, making his spiritual leadership almost non-existent. His sons, because their father did not call them to account, only compounded the issue. The people grew disdainful of all things religious. The prophet (Samuel) was recognized, but no one listened to

his counsel. So, when Israel went to war, things didn't go well. Why? They forgot to bring God! But bringing the Ark to war because when the Ark was present in the past, battles were won and rivers opened was not the answer.

Israel had it all: experience, history, the law, and a prophet, yet failed to be successful because they were missing a crucial ingredient—God Himself. Before we shake our heads at how they could be so misguided, let's pause and recognize the challenge to us. When we do, we may find this story a bit more uncomfortable and closer to home.

How often do we charge out in the name of God whether as an individual, a church, school, or business because we believe it's what God wants us to do when in actuality it's what we want to do? We think we should go to the mission field or marry this person or take this job. We decide this is what God wants us to do when what we may really be doing is seeking something for ourselves. We add some prayer, we find a few choice texts, and we throw in a few signs when what we may actually be doing is not following God but telling Him to follow us.

Please recognize that I'm not casting aspersions on God's calling. He does and He will. But what I'm suggesting is that a relationship with God must come first. We must study deeply into His Word, listen to His prophets, and learn His voice. These allow us to know He is leading as we step out in faith to follow Him versus our deciding something is a good idea and then finding a way to place God in it to make it so.

Bringing the Ark onto the battlefield didn't bring God, but only a symbol making God more like a lucky charm. If we are honest, we can also fall into the same temptation. Pray. Study His Word. Meditate on His promises. Read His prophets. As you do, God's plan will be revealed, the one He desires and not the other way around. God first, then us. In this, we will be renewed.

> **Bringing the Ark onto the battlefield didn't bring God, but only a symbol making God more like a lucky charm.**

FURTHER READING

Patriarchs and Prophets, pages 582-589

The Story of Redemption, pages 185-191

The Bible Story, vol. 3, pages 155-159

Renew YOUR SPIRIT

make new • restore • replenish • reestablish • revive

`DIGGING DEEPER`

In contrast with Israel, the Philistines paid more reverence and respect toward God. Interestingly, despite the incredible evidence that God was superior in every way to Dagon, their god, they didn't acknowledge Him. This leads us to the same lesson, but from a different direction.

> The evidence was overwhelming that God is God. And yet, the Philistines didn't accept what was right before their eyes.

The Ark was placed in Dagon's temple. In the morning Dagon was found in a position of supplication, on the floor as if in worship to God. The next morning after having been restored to his position, Dagon was found again on the floor this time smashed and scattered.

The Ark was sent from one principle Philistine city to another, where, in each case, the same thing happened—a plague broke out and mice overtook the fields and granaries. The Philistines got the message. This God is powerful. They even did as Israel should have. They went to their spiritual leaders for counsel and followed the counsel to the letter! The cows left their newborn calves willingly in yokes they had never been trained to use on a road they had never seen. The evidence was overwhelming that God is God. And yet, the Philistines didn't accept what was right before their eyes.

So, one side, the believers (Israel), added God to their plans hoping He would approve. The nonbelievers (Philistines) had God, respected His power, but failed to recognize Him as God.

Which camp are we? Neither is great. One takes their own counsel and hopes God will bless. The other doesn't accept God for who He is. Plan this week to discover who God is and what He has in store for you and follow His plan.

A relationship with God must come *first*.

> **MAKING IT REAL**

My six-year-old grandson is into treasure maps. He likes to hide "treasure" in my house and then draws an elaborate map to find each item.

Why not draw a God map this week. First, remember some ways that God has blessed you. Maybe you were protected from an accident; blessed by family; saved from something; or discovered something that changed your life. Write them down and then create a map that shows God's leading.

Once you're finished, share your map with your family. Hang it up on the refrigerator or bathroom mirror where you can look at it for several days. Let it help you know that God is leading you each day.

WEEK FORTY-EIGHT

Wanting to Be Like Others

READ **1 SAMUEL 8-10**

1 Samuel 8:5 *"Look, you are old, and your sons do not walk in your ways. Now make us a king to judge us like all the nations."*

RENEW YOUR MIND

When I was a little girl there was something I wanted more than anything—a station wagon. I don't mean one for my dolls, but a real one. You see, I was an only child with a single mom. I always felt I was standing outside a candy store looking in the window, face pressed to the glass, meaning that I was aware our two-person family was quite different from everyone else's. Others had two parents and enough kids to fill a station wagon. So, in my eight-year-old mind, if we could only have a station wagon, we'd be like everyone else.

Israel also stood at the proverbial candy store window. They weren't looking at families, but nations that, to them, seemed strong, powerful, and wealthy. Those nations had one thing in common—a king. So, it stood to reason that if Israel had a king, they would be all those things as well. But Israel's short-sightedness went further than just appearances. They wanted a king who would fight on their behalf, win their wars, conquer their enemies, and ultimately bring tribute into their treasury (1 Sam. 8:20).

As an adult, I look back at my childish desire and recognize the foolishness of wanting a station wagon. As for looking into the candy store, I've since learned that even candy stores can be too much of a good thing. Having family is wonderful, but it also comes with challenges.

Notice that Israel doesn't ask about the idea of having a king but demands it (v. 5). All of Samuel's objections did not dissuade them. God gave them a long list of reasons why it wasn't a good idea, but they pushed forward their idea in spite of

His warnings. How interesting that God granted them the desire of their heart knowing full well it wasn't the best direction.

This becomes a lesson for us—several in fact. First, be satisfied with the blessings you have. Next, listen to counsel and count the costs. Last, and most importantly, listen to God and allow Him to lead. If you study the Old Testament you will discover that God wasn't actually opposed to a king. A king for Israel was foretold long before this, but the plan needed to unfold in God's time with His purpose (see Gen. 17:6, 16; 49:10; Ex. 19:6; Num. 24:17-19; Deut. 17:14-20].

Following God can be difficult. It is tempting to look over fences, into windows, and across cubicles to want what others have. But you will find renewal when you look into your heart and discover the blessings you have right in front of you each day.

> **How interesting that God granted them the desire of their heart knowing full well it wasn't the best direction.**

FURTHER READING

Patriarchs and Prophets, pages 589-612

The Bible Story, vol. 3, pages 160-169

Renew YOUR SPIRIT

make new • restore • replenish • reestablish • revive

DIGGING DEEPER

My mother never did buy that station wagon I wanted so desperately. She recognized what I did not. First, we didn't need a car that big, and second, two people sitting in a car made for six or more would only make us feel smaller.

Interestingly, God, our Heavenly Parent, knew that the demand that Israel made for a king was also unwise, but He allowed them to move forward anyway. Yes, He offered counsel through Samuel as to why it wasn't a good idea, and that more grief would come from the decision than good, but God allowed them to move forward. But why? If God knew it was a bad decision, why be supportive?

Because it points to the very reason we are in this great controversy between good and evil. God does not force Himself on man. Man is allowed a choice. Guidance is given through His Word and His prophets. God foretells the consequences but allows us to choose our own way. More importantly, God does not abandon us even when we think we know best. Israel made a mistake in going with a king. It was a full rejection of God, but He did not abandon them. What amazing love He has for us, that even in our sin, He stays with us and when we cry for help, He's immediately there to help, guide, and accept.

MAKING IT REAL

For worship today, read Psalm 139:7-13, aloud. Study these verses and if alone, think about what they are saying about God when we make choices that go against Him. If with others or your family, discuss this attribute of God. **How meaningful is it that God is with you no matter what?**

Discover
the blessings you
have right in front
of you each day.

WEEK FORTY-NINE

King Saul Becomes Proud

> **READ** **1 SAMUEL 11-15**

1 Samuel 13:13 And Samuel said to Saul, "You have done foolishly. You have not kept the commandment of the Lord your God, which He commanded you. For now the Lord would have established your kingdom over Israel forever."

> **RENEW YOUR MIND**

One summer my family took a trip to Vancouver, British Columbia. We visited Capilano Suspension Bridge Park. As its name suggests, the main attraction is a suspension bridge that hangs between two points high above the Capilano River. I have a fear of heights, and more specifically bridges over water, so this wasn't what I would call a fun excursion.

At first, Saul demonstrates a level of humility as we find him hiding in the baggage or farming as if nothing major had changed his life. He demonstrates courage and faith as he leads Israel against the Ammonites. But what follows for Saul is a struggle of faith versus fear.

When we arrived at the bridge site, my plan was to wait for my group to walk the bridge and return. But the way the park is arranged, the suspension bridge is the entry to most of what you will experience. To not cross the bridge, would mean you would have paid admission for nothing other than a view of the gift shop. I was faced with a bridge over water that swayed not only back and forth, but up and down. Fear was absolutely present.

Saul was to meet Samuel in a week's time. Together they would move the kingdom forward as God directed. But Saul was afraid. His enemies were great. His weapons were few. His fear spread to his troops and added another problem—desertion. That's what fear does—it either holds you where you are, or you run as fast as you can in the opposite direction.

I would have run if I could, but it wasn't an option. Staying in one place didn't seem to be a smart choice either. I could say my fear spread to my group, but that wasn't the case. Instead, the adults were having a bit of sport at my dilemma with some fairly unhelpful suggestions. That's when I felt a small hand take mine. I looked down to see my six-year-old grandson's face looking up at me. "I'll take you across, Grammie," he said. "I'll get you there safely. Just hold my hand."

All of us encounter fear or worry. If we like Saul, focus on what we don't have or become overwhelmed by our problems, fear will take hold and cause us to either get stuck or make unwise choices. Faith, on the other hand, is remembering that Jesus stands next to us and quietly takes our hand. He says, "I'll get you there safely. Just focus on me."

I did make it over that bridge. True to his word, my grandson held my hand and while I won't say I wasn't afraid, I put my faith and trust in a little boy's love. When you do the same with Jesus, you will face your own fears and be renewed.

> **That's what fear does—it either holds you where you are, or you run as fast as you can in the opposite direction.**

FURTHER READING

Patriarchs and Prophets, pages 612-631

The Bible Story, vol. 3, pages 170-185

Renew YOUR SPIRIT

make new • restore • replenish • reestablish • revive

DIGGING DEEPER

A very serious lesson for us is found in these chapters that trace the beginning of Saul's kingship over Israel. We find it in the story where Samuel gave Saul the opportunity to demonstrate his loyalty to God. Samuel gave Saul specific instructions related to the attack on Amalekites.

> Saul followed God's orders through Samuel, but in his own way.

This is a tough story for us to understand in the twenty-first century. God specifically directed Saul to lead Israel to completely destroy the Amalekites and everything in their city. The Hebrew word used here is *cherem*, which means "to consecrate to God." Saul was given specific directions. He was told to *cherem* the Amalekites (dedicate them to God) by "slaying them" (1 Sam. 15:21). In other words, they were dedicated for destruction.

The lesson comes when we see that Saul followed God's orders through Samuel, but in his own way. He allowed Israel to keep the best of the animals in order to do a bit of a "trade." Israel substituted their own less valuable animals with the Amalekite flocks and herds. God would get His share, but the people would benefit too.

Saul also did his own interpretation of God's instructions by not killing Agag. Saul probably had no intention of keeping Agag alive. He had no use for him, with one exception. Agag was a valuable war trophy. To parade him among the Israelites or other surrounding nations was a way to gain back what he'd lost previously. Agag was how Saul would demonstrate his military prowess to the people. He'd then kill him later. In his mind, he rationalized no differently than his people. *I'm following what God said but doing it better—in my own way.*

I'm sure you see the lesson. We can be tempted to do the same. We read God's Word and have every intention of following it, but we sometimes do it in a way to gain something for ourselves. After all, God gets what He wants, we get what we want—is there a problem? There is! As soon as we get to a place where we begin to convince ourselves that compromise to God's law is acceptable, we are in dangerous territory. We've opened the door to Satan and his twisting of God and thus begins a slippery slope into sin we never thought or anticipated.

You can place all of your faith and trust in *Him.*

MAKING IT REAL

For family worship, talk about Saul's story. Then take time to "rewrite" it. Identify where he made poor choices and decide what he could have done instead. If you have children in your family, make this a time to emphasize how choices make a difference. Particularly help them to understand that some choices have eternal consequences.

WEEK FIFTY

God Chooses a New King

READ **1 SAMUEL 16**

1 Samuel 16:7 *"For the Lord does not see as man sees; for man looks at the outward appearance, but the Lord looks at the heart."*

RENEW YOUR MIND

For the Lord does not see as man sees; for man looks at the outward appearance, but the Lord looks at the heart" (1 Samuel 16:7). These are familiar words. And we understand the message: Just because someone looks good, it may not reflect what is really going on inside.

Saul was chosen by God because he looked the part. People saw his height, his bearing, and instantly imagined a king. Samuel looked at Jesse's eldest son, Eliab, who was tall and handsome, and made the same mistake. Two men, both handsome, but the wrong choice. We get it. God wasn't looking on the outside, but the inside.

Enter David. How was he described? Ruddy, handsome, with beautiful eyes—another good-looking person! Yet, there seems to be a difference.

When Samuel asked Jesse whether he has another son, note several things:
- Jesse didn't reference David by name.
- David wasn't invited to the feast.
- David would never have been invited had Samuel not insisted.
- David was doing a job normally given to a servant.

This seems unusual. David was handsome, so others should be attracted to him, as they were to Saul and Eliab. Why was he treated differently by his family?

Depending on the commentary you read, there are any number of speculations. We know David was young. We don't know his age, but it is suggested he could have been anywhere between ages 10 to 15 when this occurred. He was described as "ruddy," or "red." Again, pure speculation, but some believe his skin tone might have been markedly different—perhaps paler, demonstrating some sunburn or just the opposite, much darker tan, due to frequent exposure to the sun. Another suggestion is that he might have been from a secondary wife or concubine, meaning he not have been fully recognized as Jesse's son—yes, biologically, but not in the true line of descendants.

These suggestions potentially expand the meaning of verse 7. Outward appearance isn't referencing only beautiful people, but also those who are marginalized for no fault of their own—their birth, race, age, or gender. How often are we set aside or overlooked for reasons we cannot change? Or should we ask the harder question: how often have we done the same to someone else?

Obviously, the biggest takeaway is that God looks past all of this and sees the heart. No matter his appearance or how others saw him, David's heart was different. His time shepherding, experiencing God's creation, was complemented by a heart open to God's leading and the whispers of the Spirit. We know this because of what David did after he was anointed, a significant and unexpected life event. He went back to the field. He didn't boast of being better than his brothers. He didn't calculate the best way to overthrow Saul and take the throne. He simply went back to work. He went back to being David, no different to his family than when he arrived at the feast, yet he was different to God.

God sees us as we are and recognizes what we can become. God needs you in spite of your appearance or circumstances. We don't need to be famous. We don't need to be important. We don't need to be powerful. We don't need to carry great responsibilities or be called for leadership. And we should state the obvious—we don't need to be good-looking by man's measurements. We simply need to have hearts completely open to Him, ready to serve, learn, commit, and be renewed. And might I add, it's actually what a "beautiful" person looks like.

> **Outward appearance isn't referencing only beautiful people, but also those who are marginalized for no fault of their own—their birth, race, age, or gender.**

FURTHER READING

Patriarchs and Prophets, pages 631-644

The Bible Story, vol. 3, pages 185-192

Renew YOUR SPIRIT

make new • restore • replenish • reestablish • revive

> **DIGGING DEEPER**

In the last part of 1 Samuel 16, we discover that David was well-known for his music. He's called to Saul's tents to play his harp and sing as a way to soothe Saul. David lifted his voice in song and acknowledged God, and it's through this that Saul's evil spirit left and offered him rest.

> This is the beginning of the rise of David, blessed by God, and the decline of Saul, who has turned away from God.

Something key happens in chapter 16 between verses 13 and 14. In verse 13, we read that the Spirit of the Lord came upon David, while in verse 14, we read that the Spirit of the Lord left Saul. This is the beginning of the rise of David, blessed by God, and the decline of Saul, who has turned away from God.

The challenge in the text is that what troubled Saul is often translated an "evil spirit" that originates from God. This isn't actually the best translation. It should be read as an injurious or troubling spirit, which we might equate today to depression, moodiness, or gloominess. As Saul's story unfolds, it would seem he is exceedingly troubled leading him to make unwise, rash, and senseless decisions.

Thus, we are able to see how a walk with God with a mind centered on Him benefits us in blessings of encouragement, strength, and power as opposed to being independent of the mind and plans of God.

God sees us as we are and recognizes what *we can become*.

MAKING IT REAL

Music is known as a powerful influence over our minds. Thus, it's important when choosing music that it is uplifting and encouraging. Here are a few ways you and/or your family can use music during worship time. These can be done as one person alone or with others. Note how you feel before you begin and how you feel when you are finished. I believe you will see that the Spirit is able to penetrate the heart and mind through hymns and songs.

1. **We don't know what psalms David might have composed** as a teenager tending his flock, but we do know that he brought his experiences into his psalms. Take time to read one of these Psalms each day: Psalm 8, 19, 23, 29. Read the Psalm aloud and imagine it being sung. You could choose one Psalm and read the same one each day, but from a different translation.

2. **Are you musical? Here's a challenge for you this week.** We have the lyrics of the psalm, but not the music. Compose a tune for Psalm 23. Practice it each day. Teach it to your family or let the family help in the creation. Sing the psalm for worship at the end of the week.

3. **Each day, select a hymn** from the *Seventh-day Adventist Hymnal*. Read the hymn aloud—don't sing it. Hymns are like psalms. Concentrate only on the lyrics. At the end of the week have a sing-along and sing the hymns you read during the week.

WEEK FIFTY-ONE

David and Goliath

READ 1 SAMUEL 17; 18:1-9

1 Samuel 17:33 And Saul said to David, "You are not able to go against this Philistine to fight with him; for you are a youth, and he a man of war from his youth."

RENEW YOUR MIND

I know someone with an amazing talent. You won't find it on the typical list: singing, drawing, or athletic ability. This individual can see what isn't there but will be. Let me give an example.

Recently she found a used hallway table. It wasn't old enough to be an antique or new enough to be trending. It was one of those pieces of furniture that when you see it, you simply look past it.

But she saw its potential. She removed the veneer, sanded the entire piece, and refinished it to perfection. It now stands in her home, completely transformed and unrecognizable from its first appearance. Who knew this ordinary table could become extraordinary? What she saw was what most of us struggle with—seeing possibilities.

1 Samuel 8-17 repeatedly presents the same lesson: God sees in ways we do not. First, people saw Saul as a king, but he proved unworthy of the task. Next, no one,

including Samuel, saw David as a king, yet God chose him. Now, David arrived at Israel's military encampment just as Goliath stepped out on the field of battle.

Israel saw a giant of a man and a serious personal threat. Day after day Goliath called someone—anyone—out to battle. The persistent and continual insults led first to embarrassment, then to shame, and finally to despair, because there was no response. Not from the soldiers. Not from the captains. Not from the king.

David, though, was immediately incensed because of what he saw. Notice it is different than everyone else. Everyone described Goliath as "this man," (1 Samuel 17:24), while David (verse 25) saw him in spiritual terms—"this uncircumcised Philistine." Do you hear the difference? They saw a threat to themselves. David saw a worshiper of lifeless idols speaking against "the living God." David had learned to see what God sees—the heart.

Goliath is described in great detail from his height to his armor to the size and weight of his spear. David, in contrast, is only pictured again as a youth, ruddy, and good-looking. Big against small. Experience against youth. Arrogance against indignation. Undeterred, David saw what was possible—a mighty warrior would be conquered by a God-directed stone hurled from the pocket of an ordinary sling.

The person I referenced doesn't see only furniture with potential, but people as well. I think she may have seen it in her husband, who had a history of being an unruly teenager and young adult but is now a passionate man for God. She's also training her children to see differently. How? By enlisting their help in making treasures out of things that others saw only as trash. One day her children, whose eyes are being trained to see past appearances, will also apply it to people and this newfound eyesight will change their world.

How are you seeing today? It takes time. It takes practice. But like David, we too can see as God sees. When we do, we are renewed.

> David saw a worshiper of lifeless idols speaking against "the living God." David had learned to see what God sees—the heart.

FURTHER READING

Patriarchs and Prophets, pages 644-650

The Bible Story, vol. 4, pages 9-13

Renew YOUR SPIRIT

make new • restore • replenish • reestablish • revive

DIGGING DEEPER

The story of David is well-known and possibly told more than any other from the Bible. Everyone, both Christian and non-Christian, seems to be able to relate to the little guy going up against the giant. It's easy to apply this to everyday life or to the society around us.

> Because David was focused on God and fueled by his righteous indignation, he stood for God alone when no one else did.

But to do so and move on would be to miss some of the more important lessons within this story. Consider these three lessons:

1. The first is obviously appearance—God asks us to look upon the heart. David saw Goliath as a threat to God and His people. Interestingly the narrator tells the story using the Hebrew word that can be used for either "hand" or "paw" (verse 37). David saw Goliath no differently than the lion or the bear that attacked his flock.
2. David's confidence stands in marked contrast to everyone else. Because David was focused on God and fueled by his righteous indignation, he stood for God alone when no one else did. When was the last time you stood on God's behalf? There are times today when God is maligned, His name misappropriated, or His sanctuary defiled. Will you stand for Him even if you are alone?
3. David was undeterred in his quest to vanquish Goliath. It never occurred to David that Goliath would not be conquered. We also need to move forward with holy boldness on God's behalf.
4. David fought Goliath on his own terms. He was not persuaded to fight in Saul's armor or to use the traditional methods. He went up against Goliath in a way he felt most comfortable. The lion and the bear were challenging, but now it can be seen that they were life experiences that bolstered David's ability to slay the bigger foe. Life throws curve balls and we sometimes wonder, "why me?" It may be that God is preparing you for an even bigger event where you need to stand on His behalf.

We can learn to see as *God sees.*

MAKING IT REAL

David and Goliath is a great story and one that you should celebrate during family worship this week. Here are some ideas for each day:

1. **Sunday:** Memorize what David said to Goliath (1 Sam. 17:45). Repeat the memory verse each day.
2. **Monday:** Figure out how big Goliath was by laying on the floor and measuring out the length. If there are several children, line up head to toe until you are as big as Goliath.
3. **Tuesday:** Sing "Only a Boy Named David" complete with the motions.
4. **Wednesday:** Act out the story with someone playing David, Saul, soldiers, and, of course, Goliath. Use the memory verse at the appropriate time.
5. **Thursday:** Goliath was big. David was small. Can you identify something or someone bigger than you that makes life hard?
6. **Friday:** Goliath represented someone who was against God and those who follow Him. What kind of "enemies" do we face who are like Goliath?
7. **Sabbath:** David chose five stones. What tools does God give you to fight the enemy?

WEEK FIFTY-TWO

What Jealousy Does

READ 1 SAMUEL 18:9-16; 19:1-21; 22:1-23; 24:1-25:1

1 Samuel 18:12 Now Saul was afraid of David, because the Lord was with him, but had departed from Saul.

RENEW YOUR MIND

Christmas in our home is a time to share gifts. I have to admit I love this! I take great joy in finding just the right gift that will light up someone's eyes.

One particular Christmas when the girls were about middle school age, I had delayed wrapping the gifts until Christmas Eve. As I dug into my task I quickly realized I had forgotten to buy tags. Now I could have made some homemade tags, but it was late, I was tired, and I thought, *This could be a new way to do Christmas. I'll wrap the presents with no tags on them. I most likely will remember which is which and even if I don't, it will still be fun!*

It was memorable, but for all the wrong reasons. We still half smile and half roll our eyes remembering the Christmas with no tags. *No one* selected the right gift from under the tree. So, when they unwrapped the gift with great expectations, they were met with disappointment as they recognized it wasn't for them and had to turn it over to someone else. It was particularly a bad idea when you have two girls close in age. They'd open a gift, exclaim, "What I always wanted!" and then I would say, "Oh, that's not yours, it's your sister's." Needless to say, the spirit of Christmas didn't last long in our house that morning. It went from grumbling to irritation to flat out unhappiness.

A spirit of discontentment descended on King Saul. As David moved into the palace and became more and more successful, Saul grew more and more disgruntled. At first, Saul saw David as charming, with a temperament that soothed the king's soul. But as people continued to sing David's praises, the more Saul's jealousy grew eventually to the point where Saul attempted to take David's life at least four different times.

While our home on that Christmas morning never reached that level of seriousness, it doesn't take much to nurture an unkind spirit. When we focus on how things are not going well; when we compare ourselves to others; when we continually look for ways to set ourselves up to look better; when we stop giving and think only about receiving—it is then that discontentment can take root and grow until it pushes away the kind and gentle Spirit that Jesus wants to bring to our hearts.

Certainly, there are times when things won't be going well, much like realizing none of the presents are yours and everyone else's seem better. It's okay to acknowledge disappointment. But after we do, let's lift our eyes away from ourselves. Think of Jesus. Think of our blessings. Replenish your spirit and be renewed.

> It's okay to acknowledge disappointment.

FURTHER READING

Patriarchs and Prophets, pages 650-664

The Bible Story, vol. 4, pages 14-40

Renew YOUR SPIRIT

make new • restore • replenish • reestablish • revive

DIGGING DEEPER

Saul and David were two men with vastly different experiences, but both made mistakes. David ran from Saul and made two critical errors—the first at Nob and the second at Gath. Saul ordered the killing of 85 priests, including the High Priest. What made the sin even more grievous was that Doeg, Saul's henchman, went on to wipe out the entire town of Nob, save one.

> David made some serious errors which from all appearances seemed as if he had abandoned God.

David made some serious errors which from all appearances seemed as if he had abandoned God. He lied to the High Priest and sought refuge with the enemy (nonbelievers). Remember, all through David's early life we have been shown that God recognizes not what is seen on the outside, but the heart, where one's true allegiance lies.

If we layer the Psalms David wrote on top of this part of his life, we will discover that while David may have appeared to be abandoning God, in actuality he saw God with Him the entire time. Even when it appeared that David was running in an opposite direction, the Psalms reveal his heart.

Read these verses to describe what was happening to David and then the psalm he wrote in response.

1 Samuel 19:12-18   Psalm 59
1 Samuel 21:10-15   Psalm 34
1 Samuel 22:1, 2   Psalm 57
1 Samuel 23:29   Psalm 142

MAKING IT REAL

If you haven't taken the time to read any of the Psalms above, choose one or two to read. Then compose your own psalm (at least the words) that reflects your journey with God.

Let us
lift our eyes
away from ourselves.

About the Author

Merle Poirier writes from Silver Spring, Maryland, where she works as the operation manager for *Adventist Review* and *Adventist World* magazines as well as the designer for *KidsView*, a magazine for 8-12-year-olds. She enjoys spending time with her family including being the grandmother of two active little boys, who greatly enjoy Starting With Jesus.

About the Designer

Ellen Musselman lives in Silver Spring, Maryland, with her husband and two boys. She has been a designer for more than 15 years. She currently works as the senior designer for Types & Symbols, a creative studio dedicated to presenting Adventism beautifully. She enjoys the busyness of life being at home with two young boys, while squeezing in time for design when all are asleep. This project has been a special one, as it combines her passions for design and ministry, all while working alongside her mother, the one who first introduced her to design many years ago.